PRAIS

Few Americans are aware that Ale   , has two books among the most popular in American history–his collaboration with Malcolm X and *Roots*. Adam Henig underscores this point and more in his brief but incisive biography of Haley. Much more can be said about this magnificent writer and if Henig's book doesn't ignite this search, it will stand as a worthy pursuit of Haley's contribution to American letters. –Herb Boyd, author of *Baldwin's Harlem: A Biography of James Baldwin* and co-editor of *By Any Means Necessary: Malcolm X: Real, Not Reinvented*

***

Some critics accused Alex of making up significant portions of *Roots*. Did he? Henig tackles this touchy question head on. Result: A highly readable story. –Edward T. Thompson, Editor-in-Chief, *Reader's Digest*, 1976-1984.

***

Adam Henig has created a gem....A must read for anyone interested in the interplay of politics, race and mixed blessings of fame and fortune that produced the contradictory legacy of a onetime icon. –Terry P. Wilson, Professor Emeritus of Ethnic Studies, UC Berkeley

***

Henig's writing is sharp, brisk and clear. [He] cuts through all the dense details to keep the story moving forward. –Tony Platt, Visiting Professor, San Jose State University

***

Henig takes us on a fascinating journey through Alex Haley's life...and shows us how Haley's life was turned upside down by the sudden and overwhelming success of both the book and the miniseries. –*Mark My Words Blog*

***

While this 52 page book may be his first, it represents a major literary achievement. This book may renew scholar and the general public's interest in Roots once again. –Nvasekie Konneh, *Black Star News*

ALEX HALEY'S ROOTS

ALEX HALEY'S ROOTS

An Author's Odyssey

ADAM HENIG

Cover designed by Rachmad Agus of RAC Design

For
Jennifer
Jacob and Alex
and my parents
Gerald and Lori Henig

CONTENTS

ROOTSMANIA

SUNDAY, JANUARY 23, 1977

Neither man uttered a word. Inside his suite at the Pierre Hotel on Fifth Avenue in New York City, actor Warren Beatty looked over at his fifty-five-year-old friend, Alex Haley. The two-hour television premiere of *Roots*, adapted from Haley's best-selling book, had just ended. The credits were rolling.

"Did you have any idea, any dream of all this?" Beatty asked.

"If I had, I'd have typed a whole lot faster," the writer quipped in his deep baritone Southern drawl.

Beatty, who had met Haley a few years earlier through their film agent, remarked prophetically, "Your life will never be the same again. "

The following evening at Lincoln Center's Avery Fisher Hall, Haley was scheduled to deliver a talk on the same stage on which the New York Philharmonic Orchestra performed. Before the doors opened, Haley stepped onto the stage to survey the three-thousand-seat auditorium. It wasn't the first time he'd spoken at a venue of this size, but this one was certainly the most impressive. Though the audiences and venues changed, the topic never did.

Haley's talk was always about his work-in-progress, a genealogical account spanning more than two centuries. The story began with Haley's great-great-great-great-grandfather, Kunta Kinte, a West African captured by slave traders. It followed Kunta Kinte's life in bondage and the lives of his descendants. Based on stories Haley had first heard from his grandmother as a youngster on her front porch in Henning, Tennessee, *Roots: The Saga of an American Family*, would take twelve years, two editors, and a failed marriage to complete.

What inspired Haley to pen a book about his ancestry took hold during his early years as a freelance writer. In 1959, after serving two decades in the US Coast Guard—the latter half spent as the coast guard's chief journalist—Haley had relocated to Greenwich Village, a popular destination at the time for struggling artists, musicians, and, of course, writers. Barely able to afford three meals a day, the five-foot-nine, pudgy thirty-eight-year-old at first struggled. No longer living on a military salary nor able to draw from his pension (his first wife, whom he was separated from, and their two children were living off of it), Haley had reached a low point.

One evening, he took stock of his entire net worth, as he later put it, "two cans of sardines and eighteen cents."

Ever the optimist, Haley was determined to make a name for himself. With the aid of an established writer (James Baldwin), a supportive editor (*Reader's Digest*'s Fulton Oursler, Jr.), and a savvy literary agent (Paul R. Reynolds), the ex-coast guardsman honed his skills and eventually went from a second-rate journalist to one of the leading black writers for popular magazines such as *Reader's Digest*, *Playboy*, *Saturday Evening Post*, and

Haley's big break came when he coauthored the best-selling 1965 memoir, *The Autobiography of Malcolm X*. Though Haley had little sympathy for Malcolm X's radical ideas, the author recognized how these ideas were shaped by the tragic legacy of American slavery, a story yet to be told properly to the mainstream. What finally convinced Haley to take on the task came during an assignment for *Playboy* in London.

During the turbulent sixties, the men's magazine hired Haley as a freelancer. His job was to interview celebrities for the popular "Interview" feature. Having already interviewed Malcolm X, Miles Davis, and Rev. Martin Luther King Jr., his latest subject was British actress Julie Christie. Visiting Christie outside of London on the set of *Darling*, Haley had no luck luring the film star away. Instead, he passed the time at the renowned British Museum, where he encountered the two-thousand-year-old Rosetta Stone. Mesmerized, he discovered that the stone he was hovering over had "unlocked" the past to ancient Egypt. It was at that moment, Alex Haley recalled, the journey of discovering his roots began.

That evening at the Lincoln Center, Haley spoke for two hours. He never stopped to pause or take a sip from his water glass. Afterward, overwhelmed by fans, Haley did something that would become part of a ritual. He snuck out the back door. He was driven to two high-end parties sponsored by Doubleday, his publisher. It was a heady experience for a man who, some fifteen years before, was unemployed and living in a basement on the opposite end of town.

The next day, following a lunchtime lecture at the Dutch Treat Club (a men's civic organization), Haley returned to his hotel room to find scores of books to be signed, not to mention four people waiting for him: a friend from the Carnegie Foundation, a photographer, a reporter, and a representative from Gambia (his protagonist's native country). Haley's daily routine would not let up. Everywhere Haley went—New England, the Midwest, and the South—well-wishers greeted him. His cab driver from JFK Airport was "thrilled to be driving the newly famous writer." Back in Manhattan, walking the beat, a black NYPD officer grabbed the author's hand. "Hey, brother, that's a magnificent piece of work. You've made us all proud."

By the end of the eight-night, twelve-hour miniseries, which the *New York Times* proclaimed the "most significant civil rights event since the Selma-to-Montgomery march of 1965," the man behind *Roots* had become America's newest folk hero.

For eight straight nights, the nation stopped what it was doing. Americans hadn't just been watching TV; they'd been caught up in a broadcast phenomenon. Hospitals in New York City reported a "drastic drop" in the number of admissions while the series aired. The NYPD observed a mysterious, ghost-like feel to the city's streets. Across the nation, the timing of even the most mundane activities was shaped by the television show. In Winston-Salem, North Carolina, for example, a Boy Scout meeting was rescheduled to accommodate *Roots*, while in Atlanta, a church shortened its choir practice for the same reason. At Cleveland State University, a professor offered a mid-week seminar to discussthe miniseries. Expecting a dozen students, he found two hundred waiting for him.

Although the blizzard of January 1977 (which covered two-thirds of the nation and was one of the worst since the US Weather Service began keeping records) may have increased viewer numbers, it certainly was not the sole reason for the series' unprecedented audience size. Out west, where the temperature was more cooperative, viewership was equally as impressive. From coast to coast, restaurants, movie theaters, and nightclubs reported a sharp decline in customers. Even in Las Vegas, casinos were virtually empty and shows were rescheduled. By week's end, seven of the eight episodes were included in the top ten spots for most-watched television programs *ever*. The final episode reached eighty million viewers, an all-time record. Black and white, rich and poor, young and old, urban and rural residents were all caught up in "Rootsmania."

After only one week of celebrity, Haley already missed his quiet days as a private citizen. He was used to spending weeks or months holed up in a hotel room with just a typewriter. In his Manhattan hotel room, he was hoping to catch up on some much needed sleep before flying to Los Angeles, but he was soon interrupted by a knock on the door. The nightstand clock read 3:30 a.m. He closed his eyes and tried to go back to sleep. The knocking continued. Reluctant to get out of bed but concerned there might be an emergency, Haley answered the door in his underwear. A white bellhop extended his hand. "Sir," the young man said, "I want to thank you for what you've done for America."

A few hours later, Haley was standing outside of a terminal at JFK Airport when a skycap did a double take. "Alex Haley," the skycap yelled. Nearby passengers came over to see what the commotion was about. The crowd swelled in numbers, jostling for a glimpse, then began pushing and shoving, hoping to obtain autographs. Haley's plane was due to leave and he had lost sight of his luggage.

"That's him! That's him!" The unruly crowd grabbed at his clothes and limbs. The women were worse than the men. Buttons began popping off his shirt. Rescue came in the form of a red-jacketed American Airlines employee who parted the swarming crowd and led the author with baggage in tow to a private airport entrance and to his plane. He suggested that Haley upgrade his seat to first class.

In Los Angeles, the writer's first stop was the suburb of Culver City, where he was slated to sign books inside the recently completed Fox Hills Mall. At $12.50 per book (expensive for a hardcover in 1977), the mall's bookstore was anticipating a lucrative afternoon. Haley had allocated two hours for the signing before leaving for his next engagement—an appearance on *The Tonight Show Starring Johnny Carson.*

Entering the employee entrance, he heard a noise above. A news helicopter was hovering. The bookstore manager informed the author that there were over three thousand people waiting, an unheard-of crowd for a book signing; the nation's best-known writers were fortunate to attract a few hundred. The line began in the bookstore and stretched through the mall walkway, looped out through the shopping center's exit doors and continued along the sidewalk. There were parents clutching their children's hands, disheveled teenagers sitting on the concrete sidewalk, white people, black people—all waited for Haley. For the next two and a half hours, Haley signed books until his hand cramped. When it was announced that the author was leaving, a large black woman came forward. "He ain't goin' nowhere!" she shouted. Haley took one look at her and sat back down. He took her multiple copies of *Roots,* signed each one, and then fled.

Delighted to be on *The Tonight Show,* Haley had a surprise for the program's host, Johnny Carson, whom he had interviewed a decade before for *Playboy.* Days earlier, Haley had contacted the Salt Lake City-based Institute of Family Research, one of the largest genealogical information centers in the country. He wanted to have Carson's roots traced. It had to be done in absolute secrecy, and he needed it in five days. Ordinarily, a search of this type took two months. The institute agreed, but it would cost Haley $45,000. With over a dozen researchers working day and night, the institute managed to trace Carson's lineage back to the sixteenth century. The research was catalogued in a four-hundred-page leather-bound tome that Haley handed Carson during the show. In a rare unscripted moment, Carson choked up.

Many viewers assumed that he had conducted the research himself. Haley made no mention of the institute.

About ninety-nine thousand copies of *Roots* sold the week after the miniseries aired on ABC. Doubleday switched to a high-speed press, doubling production. Every bookstore was out of stock. Grocery stores, pharmacies, and discount retailers, all of which mostly carried paperbacks, began distributing the best-seller in hardcover. Copies were for sale on street corners in various cities, even outside Saks Fifth Avenue in New York City. Four months after its debut, *Roots* had sold more than eight hundred thousand copies, unheard of for such a short period of time. Americans were obsessed and Haley did his best to oblige. From Dayton, Ohio, to Wichita, Kansas, and Phoenix, Arizona, to San Francisco, California, Haley crisscrossed the nation as if he were campaigning for the presidency.

Initially, Haley took his newfound celebrity status in stride. In Baltimore, a reporter observed that when Haley autographed his book, he could have easily signed only his name or maybe even just his initials and no one would have raised an eyebrow, given that nearly every book signing after the miniseries aired had resembled the Fox Hills turnout. Instead, "Mr. Haley, seated at a small table, asks for his or her name and he writes, carefully, 'The Family of Kunta Kinte sends best wishes to (name of recipient) family. Sincerely, Alex Haley'. . . . The book has immense meaning for him; now he wants that copy to mean a lot to its owner-reader."

By the end of the month, fans were becoming even more numerous and more zealous. In Philadelphia, a dozen guards were needed to protect the author. At a book signing in the nation's capital prior to Haley's arrival, those in attendance were jostling one another so much that the event was canceled. The organizer feared a riot could erupt.

When not autographing books, there were phone calls from heads of state, film producers, and fellow writers awaiting his attention. *Roots* had become a twenty-four hour, seven-day-a-week operation. Haley was never left alone. The demanding itinerary and intrusive media—not to mention concern for his personal safety—drove him to the brink of a physical and mental collapse. When he went for a check-up, his doctor was alarmed. He'd been averaging three hours of sleep a night. In February 1977, after five months on the road and a month after the series aired, Haley cancelled his next ten appearances, forfeiting an estimated $100,000 in earnings.

His absence from the spotlight didn't hurt sales. By March, *Roots* had been number one on the *New York Times* nonfiction best-seller list for more than twenty weeks, with one million copies sold. The public discussion continued unabated. The *Los Angeles Times* received numerous letters in response to the *Roots* miniseries. The *San Francisco Chronicle*'s mailbag regarding *Roots* was "heavy, courteous and civilized."

But not all the discourse was positive. A gentleman from Long Beach, California, felt that the movie would "inflame" race relations; a white housewife from Atlanta added that "blacks were just getting settled down, and this will make them angry again." David Duke, the grand wizard of the Ku Klux Klan concurred. The miniseries was inflammatory and could be used as an excuse to incite a riot. Nancy Reagan, wife of California Governor Ronald Reagan, expressed a similar view. Such negative opinions did little to stifle book sales or discourage the author, who was back on the road.

Besieged with awards and honors from small colleges, local historical societies, nationally recognized universities, and even the United States Senate, Haley found himself in a commanding position. This was reflected in his lecture fee. Whereas he was earning $3,000 per lecture before the movie aired and shortly thereafter, Haley was now receiving $4,500—nearly half the annual salary of the average American worker at the time. With an astonishing nine hundred lectures scheduled over the next two years, Haley was expected to earn over $4 million (equivalent to $14 million in 2013) in lecture fees alone. *Forbes* magazine estimated that if *Roots* was anything like *The Godfather*, another recent best-seller adapted into a movie, Haley was on track to amass more than $10 million (equal to $35 million in 2013). Given that potential earning power, "Haley is one author, who won't end his day in a garret," *Forbes* predicted. He clearly needed to upgrade his business operation.

For Haley, local mom-and-pop bookshop signings were becoming a thing of the past. Auditoriums and concert halls were his venue of choice. With the help of Ofield Dukes (a former Motown Records representative who headed a public-relations agency) to control both his itinerary and brand, Alex Haley established a media empire. He was no longer just an author, Dukes explained. The PR professional envisioned an enterprise comprised of publications (articles and books), lectures, and products (movies and spoken-word records). The author would no longer promote himself. This was now a full-fledged operation that required staff, offices, and investments. To get it off the ground, Dukes asked for $10,000. Haley consented.

Thousands of letters addressed to "Alex Haley, Roots, U.S.A." arrived from all over the world. Canvas bags were piling up at Haley's Los Angeles office. The author needed a team to sort through them all. Most spoke of personal experiences or asked about tracing family history. They came from children, parents, grandparents, people of color, whites, rich, poor, academics, doctors, teachers, and so on. Some wrote soliciting favors. A small-town reporter sent Haley one of his articles hoping it would be optioned for a movie. A third-grade teacher inquired about a job. Haley's secretaries did their best to respond, sending out an average of five hundred pre-typed responses a week.

2

LEGAL
TOMFOOLERY

Roots' success was a cultural (and financial) phenomenon. It was the first time that many white Americans had read a book from a black perspective. It reignited discussion and interest in the state of race relations; introduced black history to the classroom and, for that matter, the living room; established a new success formula for a television movie series; and demonstrated that blacks had the talent to serve as leading actors in serious dramas. Roots even affected the English language. Prior to the movie, the word "roots," in reference to the past, was typically used by academics. Following the broadcast, the expression was immediately adopted by the masses, seamlessly integrated into the American lexicon.

Roots' most poignant contribution may have been to the study of genealogy. Some contended that the renewed interest in the field was inspired first by the bicentennial celebration that occurred a year earlier, and second by President Jimmy Carter's well-publicized interest in his own background. Genealogy was his hobby; Carter had traced back his family's line nearly two centuries. Although each were a contributor, it was obvious that Rootsmania was the primary catalyst.

The nation's most prominent research institution, the National Archives, where Haley's search had begun a decade earlier, noted that before the broadcast, it received a little more than seven hundred inquiries per month. Now, it averaged 2,300 letters a week, with well over a hundred visitors arriving daily to conduct research on their heritage. In a poll taken two months following the miniseries, the *New York Times* reported a vast increase in interest of family origins among Americans. City, county, state, and university libraries reported an unprecedented surge in genealogical inquiries. The genealogical division of the Mormon Church in Utah, following the broadcast, was "flooded with appeals for help from ancestor-seekers of all backgrounds at the rate of one out-of-state telephone call a minute." The private sector jumped on the *Roots* bandwagon as well. From Back-to-Africa tour groups and mail-order genealogy kits to how-to books and paid-to-hire firms to locate your family origins—even naming newborns after Kunta Kinte—the field of genealogy had been transformed.

Alex Haley had achieved fame and wealth. Hollywood

celebrities, foreign dignitaries, and the nation's most powerful leaders lined up to meet him. Whether it was hobnob-
bing with Queen Farah of Iran and President Carter at a
White House luncheon, receiving a kiss on the cheek from
actress Liz Taylor (in front of Secretary of the Navy John
Warner, husband number six) at a fundraising event, or
having Hollywood's leading star Marlon Brando beg black
comedian Dick Gregory for Alex Haley's phone number, it
would seem that Haley truly was the "most wanted man in
the nation."

When time allowed, Haley spared no expense to
indulge himself. He purchased a shiny new Mercedes (with
a customized license plate that said "Kinte"). Occasionally,
he was overly generous; after coffee with a reporter at a
diner, he left a fifty-dollar tip on a six-dollar bill.

Haley's privacy, however, was a thing of the past. The
author fell victim to his own hectic schedule. It got so bad
that the middle-aged coast guard veteran was forced to create a "phony excuse just to go to the bathroom!" If Alex
Haley thought this was the worst part of being a celebrity,
he was mistaken. Unfortunately, Haley was his own worst
enemy.

It was considered irrational, foolish, and nonsensical.
Why would Alex Haley, who had earned more than $2.5
million in royalties and who was once so poor that he
threatened to commit suicide in order to escape his credi-
tors, sue his publisher, Doubleday, $5 million? It made no
sense, especially to his longtime editor and friend, Lisa
Drew.

Drew had been with Haley since Doubleday's senior editor and elder statesmen, Ken McCormick, hired her as an assistant in the early 1960s, a time when women in the book industry had few options beyond the secretarial pool. Once it became clear to McCormick that Haley was going to take longer than expected to complete his *Roots* manuscript, he had passed Haley over to his ambitious and competent assistant, Drew. Although it was an up-and-down relationship—Drew cornering Haley on several occasions demanding copy while he did his best to avoid her, one time even skipping town—the two remained close. Haley wasn't the first to sue his publisher, but he may have been the first author to file suit with a book on the best-seller list for over twenty weeks with no signs of waning.

Haley cited three major issues. First, that the publisher severely underestimated the potential sales of *Roots*. In Doubleday's defense, there had been nothing like it before. The book was already a best seller before the movie aired. After the broadcast, Doubleday could not keep up with demand until it made the decision to switch to another printing press. The publisher had anticipated a big success, printing two hundred thousand copies prior to its release date, the largest first printing the press had ever done. But bookstores across the country had still managed to sell out. This was unprecedented and unpredictable the company argued.

Second, Haley contended that his contract was unfair. At the time he had signed it, he was deeply in debt and renegotiated the paperback rights. By signing a revised

agreement, Haley received another advance from Doubleday, totaling approximately $100,000. But there was a trade
off. He'd agreed to receive a lower royalty on the paperback
edition.

Lastly, Haley believed *Roots* had not received sufficient
publicity. Doubleday argued that it had been reluctant to
invest in advertisement until the manuscript had been
completed. But once it was on the way for a fall release, the
company insisted that it had invested more money on marketing *Roots* than any of its other books.

From the publishing industry's perspective, Haley's case
was more about renegotiating a past agreement than a contract violation. Literary agent John Hawkins, who would
eventually represent Haley as a client, claimed that the
author's Hollywood-based film agent and attorney, Lou
Blau, had encouraged the suit. To Blau, this was how you
played the game—sue one day, settle the next (or in this
case, renegotiate), and everything goes back to normal. Blau
failed to realize, Hawkins explained, that Hollywood tactics
did not always translate into other industries. The suit had
left an indelible strain in the relationship between author
and publisher.

3

MARK OTTAWAY

In the midst of Haley's legal difficulties, the country of Gambia, which Kunta Kinte had called home, had become a popular tourist attraction—especially for affluent African Americans in search of their ancestry. The tiny coastal West African nation had been propelled into the spotlight for the first time since its independence in 1965 from the United Kingdom. The Gambian government declared the village of Juffure, where Haley first had located his ancestors, as a national monument. The village, a throwback to the eighteenth century, became so popular that it had been overrun with foreigners, forcing government officials to limit the number of days the public could visit.

Recognizing a potential story, a shaggy-haired British journalist convinced his employer, The [London] Sunday Times, to cover his costs while he investigated the changes this impoverished nation had experienced since the *Roots* phenomenon began. His name was Mark Ottaway. Upon arrival, Ottaway noted that Juffure, national monument or not, looked like every other village along the Gambian River. It was as if time had stood still. Villagers lived in mud-walled huts with no windows. Paved roads, electricity, and indoor plumbing were nowhere to be seen.

Hoping Rootsmania would revitalize its lackluster economy, the Gambian government was in the process of planning to turn this village into an attractive destination. The Juffure residents, who rarely had had visitors before, were also hoping for a trickle-down effect. They all knew the protocol—greet the rich foreigners (everyone was rich in comparison to them) and walk them over to the Kinte family quarters. It wasn't the original hut of Kunta Kinte, but it was the current home of his supposed ancestors. This little finagling of the truth the British journalist expected. What he did not anticipate, after speaking with several villagers, was that Kunta Kinte, upon whom Haley had based his genealogical story, was beginning to sound questionable and possibly made up. Though Haley had admitted that the dialogue in his book was mostly fiction, the story was presumed true since the publisher itself labeled *Roots* nonfiction. The author had never discussed the validity of the timelines, locations, or characters and there were no footnotes, endnotes, or a bibliography. After conducting interviews with local villagers and government officials, Ottaway's travel assignment evolved into an exposé.

After a week of fact checking in Gambia and another in

London, Ottaway, whom the *New York Times* described as a "reporter with a reputation for integrity," uncovered "grave flaws" in the author's research. Juffure, according to Ottaway, was not a little hamlet inhabited by docile Africans during the eighteenth century as Haley inferred. Rather the village was an established European "trading post," where even the Gambians themselves took part in the slave trade.

There was more.

When Haley taught at Hamilton College, a small liberal arts school in upstate New York, he met a Gambian student, Ebou Manga, who joined him on his first trip to Gambia in 1967. Manga's father, a high-ranking government official, arranged for Haley to meet with a committee of powerful citizens assigned to help trace the author's ancestors.

When Haley returned to the United States, a telegram arrived from Gambia informing him that the committee had found Haley's ancestors. Haley caught the next flight back, met with committee members, and then traveled to Juffure by boat. At the village, Haley was introduced to an elderly man in his seventies, a "griot" (the village's chief storyteller).

Ottaway also spoke with the griot. He was savvy enough to see that the storyteller was hardly a reliable source, and he was shocked to learn that Haley had not verified any of the griot's stories. Further inquiry uncovered enough details to suggest that Kunta Kinte was a figment of Haley's imagination. Haley had shared his own theories and research with the committee in advance of his meeting with the griot in Juffure; the committee had economic motives to find a griot who would confirm Haley's story. The griot, Ottaway determined, was a man of "notorious unreliability," who had no training (traditionally received from the village's previous griot) and was known for his "playboy" lifestyle. Ottaway soon discovered that the head of the Gambian National Archives had tipped off Haley three years before *Roots* went to print, writing that he had "doubts about [Kebba] Fofana's [the griot's] reliability." Worse, Fofana's son admitted to Ottaway that his father was not a griot at all. There had been no legitimate griot in Juffure for quite some time.

Continuing on his mission, Ottaway was unable to verify the author's assertion that in 1766 slave traffickers had seized Kunta Kinte. The alleged slave ship records used to trace Kunta's whereabouts from Africa to America were not listed where Haley said they were. Ottaway sifted through documents Haley had researched years earlier but came up with nothing. There was no list of cargo in any of the records, let alone itemized details of which slaves were taken on which ship.

When interviewing the Gambian villagers about their own heritage, Ottaway grew more skeptical. He found it suspicious that none of the Gambians were able to recite or even recall any historical tales that went beyond a hundred years except for one—that of a lowly villager named Kunta Kinte.

Before *The* [London] *Sunday Times* went public with Ottaway's piece, Haley was given an opportunity to respond. Based on the reporter's recollection of the conversation, Haley admitted that his research, accumulated over the years, had become "so confusing, so obscured by contradictory statements from different sources, that he [Haley] very nearly decided to make the African section, if not the entire book, a mere historical novel." Although "neither you nor I know exactly what happened," Haley allegedly said, the story of *Roots* represented the "symbol of the fate of my people."

"Tangled Roots" was published on April 10, 1977, in *The* [London] *Sunday Times*, the same week Haley was due in London for a publicity tour in anticipation of *Roots'* UK premiere broadcast. The *New York Times* and the wire services quickly picked up the five-thousand-word article. Bombarded by the international media, Haley's response was different from the one he supposedly gave to Ottaway. "I spent twelve years doing this book," he said, "and I resent any person who is obviously opportunistic, spending seven days in Africa and then writing a story which seeks to blemish the deepest, strictest, most honest research I could do, given the materials I had to work with." In other interviews, he suggested that Ottaway was the fraud. On *Good Morning America*, Haley accused his British antagonist of "looking for a headline." He went as far as to charge Ottaway with racism. To suggest *Roots* did not occur was "like saying that Anne Frank never existed or that the whole Nazi thing was a hoax."

The archivist from the Gambian National Archives, who had expressed doubts about Haley's sources, now defended the author of *Roots*, suggesting the information that he had provided the reporter was "misconstrued." John Henrik Clarke, a leading African American historian, believed the attacks on Haley were part of a "broader attempt to demean anything Black people have to say about the slavery experience." Literary critic Herb Boyd thought Haley to be a "man of great integrity" and that Ottaway's accusations "should be relegated to obscurity."

When Ottaway publicly challenged Haley to a debate during the author's London visit, Haley agreed to take the critic "head on," but then backed out.

A diversion came at the perfect moment. Haley was asked to make a return pilgrimage to Gambia. Unlike his first visit a decade earlier, when he was an unknown writer escorted by a college student, now he was accompanied by a full-fledged entourage, including his brother George, an attorney; his brother Julius, a US Navy architect; agent Lou Blau; his public-relations representative Ofield Dukes; reporters from *People*, *Newsweek*, the *New York Times*, the *Washington Post*, and *Ebony*; and an ABC camera crew. Haley was welcomed by dancers, drummers, soldiers, and prominent members of the government. The Gambian officials were delighted to see the American media represented. Perhaps it would generate much-needed tourism dollars. For the villagers of Juffure, it proved a historic day—for many, it was the first time they had ever seen a camera, let alone one that shot video. Haley asked his younger brother Julius to construct a new mosque for the local inhabitants, many of whom were Muslim. Haley would pay for it.

On his way back to New York, while held up in customs on a layover in London, Haley was notified that he'd been awarded the Pulitzer Prize. Surrounded by journalists from the leading newspapers and magazines from back home, the media immediately demanded a response. One reporter said he uttered only three words, "I'll be damned." Another quoted him as saying, "Aw shit, baby. Ain't that incredible?"

Back in the United States, he returned to his routine of hotel rooms, book signings, and public talks. News of the prize seemed to have reduced the Ottaway incident to a hiccup. But within a week of his return, there was a new detractor.

Like Haley, Margaret Walker came from a well-to-do Southern, African American family. A professor of literature at Jackson State University in Mississippi, Walker was a black female in a profession dominated by white men. She had authored the best-selling Civil War novel, *Jubilee*, loosely based on her grandmother's life. It was quite similar to portions of *Roots*, but *Jubilee* had preceded *Roots* by a decade. Held in high regard in academic circles, Walker was largely unknown to the general public. *Jubilee*, she believed, would have attained more success had she been white like Margaret Mitchell who wrote *Gone with the Wind* or male like Alex Haley. Walker was livid about *Roots*. She was convinced that it contained parts lifted from *Jubilee*. She contacted her attorney (and son), F.J. Alexander, and pinpointed thirty-five examples that could be construed as plagiarism. Haley was soon back in court.

As the plaintiff, the burden was on Walker to prove her case; her publisher offered no support. Although Haley admitted "numerous similarities of theme, structure, and language" between the two books, his legal team made clear that it wouldn't be enough to convict him on copyright infringement. These similarities, Haley's lawyers argued, were common in books that covered similar periods or topics. *Roots* editor Lisa Drew thought the charges were "ridiculous." No matter how absurd, the Doubleday lawyer was not surprised that Haley was targeted. Every best-selling author was vulnerable, especially those "who write blockbuster books." Others came to Haley's defense. The *Washington Post* maintained that Walker's case was a stretch. A colleague of Walker's thought her suit "smacked of bitterness."

But the federal court magistrate found enough evidence to take the case to trial. Copyright infringement was not determined solely on "verbatim copying"; borrowing liberally could also be construed as infringement. Haley's defense rested on the premise that he had not read *Jubilee*, which to Walker seemed unlikely given the similar topic and amount of research he had done. Walker was confident she had a solid case. And she wasn't the only one.

4

A FORMIDABLE
OPPONENT

———∾∾∾———

Harold Courlander would prove to be a formidable oppo-
nent. With a passion for African culture, Courlander, a
Caucasian, had written more than twenty books over a
thirty-year period. Like Walker, he was popular with colleagues within the field but hardly a mainstream name.
Given his quiet persona and commitment to the discipline,
it seemed that fame was never his intention. *The African*,
published in 1967, had been his biggest success. It was
about a West African-born young man taken from his village by white Europeans and sent overseas to live as a slave
in the United States. By Courlander's standards, the book
sold well. A decade after its initial release, Courlander's

royalties from it totaled about $14,000 (equivalent today to $50,000).

Like tens of millions of other Americans, Courlander had watched the *Roots* TV miniseries. He found it an entertaining but a very inaccurate portrayal. In response to the *Roots* phenomenon and the public's growing appetite for all things African, he was invited by the Smithsonian Institution to serve on a discussion panel. To prepare, Courlander thought it was best to read the book that had ignited the craze. Immediately, he began to notice similarities with his own book—the look and feel of the characters, the mood and the overall plot.

After further investigation, Courlander was convinced that he had a case. He was aware of the potential implications—as a white man, would he be viewed as a racist? Or, like Walker, would he seem just another envious author? He was familiar with Ottaway's attempt to question Haley's research methods. An executive in the book trade advised Courlander that he was "up against something incalculably great in force. Were *Roots* to be discounted, let alone disproved, the presumed threat to blacks in America would be tangible, enormous."

Whether it was a sense of justice or his age, Courlander, seventy, decided to take a stand no matter the consequences. He passed on his findings to the nation's two most influential daily newspapers, the *Washington Post* and the *New York Times*. He hoped for an immediate response but there was none, at least not until Walker's suit hit the papers. In April 1977, when the *Washington Post* published a

piece on Courlander and the increasing scrutiny of
Roots,Haley concluded that it was "open season" on him.
He insisted he was unfamiliar with *The African*. Courlan-
der claimed that Alex Haley was not entirely truthful.

Initially, Courlander had provided a short list of examples, hardly enough to warrant a lawsuit. But soon, he and
his legal team discovered more, a lot more. Over eighty passages could be cited as borderline or outright plagiarism.
After the allegations were made and reported by the *New
York Times* on May 24, Harold Courlander filed suit in New
York against Alex Haley and Doubleday as well as *Reader's
Digest*, which had published several excerpts (and provided
financial assistance for the research) prior to the book's
release. He asked for "more than half the profits of *Roots*,"
an estimated $2.5 million ($10 million in today's dollars) on
hard-copy sales alone.

The case was far from clear-cut. Since both books had
the same chronology and focused on similar events, it was
possible that Haley had used similar primary sources (i.e., a
memoir, a diary or ship's log), information that fell under
public domain. Courlander was aware of the possibility,
even admitting that his own work might have derived from
the same documentation, but that would have to be determined.

By late spring 1977, Haley was involved in three lawsuits: the one he had filed against his publisher, and the
ones leveled against him by Walker and Courlander. Haley
did his best to downplay their importance. The public still
adored him. The trials were hardly top news stories, but

they weighed on Haley's mind and he desperately needed a distraction.

Fortunately, the state of Tennessee was planning to honor the return of their "most illustrious son." Government officials and business leaders arranged a three-day statewide celebration in late May. Various cities, big and small, would host rallies, lectures, and dinners honoring the man who, according to Southern author and journalist John Egerton, "may be the nearest thing Tennessee has had to a national hero since Sergeant Alvin York returned from World War I." The three-day festivities had been organized to revitalize the state's economy, reignite pride in its citizenry, and improve race relations with African Americans. Haley's hometown was first on the itinerary.

Henning, located fifty miles north of Memphis, had changed little since 1939, the year seventeen-year-old Haley went off to the coast guard and stopped coming to his grandmother's home for annual summer vacations. The town's population was older. Many shops and banks had closed. Most blacks had left, although there were still about a hundred in a town of eight hundred people. The train on which Haley's parents, Simon (a graduate student at Cornell University) and Bertha, had ridden home years before no longer made a stop. The last Haley family member to reside in Henning was Alex's maternal grandmother, Cynthia Palmer, who had passed away more than thirty years prior.

The town was not an ideal spot for the long weekend's kickoff point. Many shops on Main Street were boarded up and those that were not were on the brink. The seventy-year-old white mayor, who also served as the town's "lone policeman and judge," publicly referred to African Americans as "niggers." He and everyone else just wanted to be left alone. Thus far, the few curious tourists who had arrived early found a town devoid of souvenirs or hoopla. The town's welcoming sign was for retired Major League Baseball outfielder and one-time All Star, Jim Hickman. Hickman, who was white and grew up in Henning, had returned to work as a farmer.

Still, a small contingent of the town's black and liberal white residents were determined to honor the author. These supporters had envisioned Henning as the next Plains (President Jimmy Carter's hometown in Georgia). Carter's small farming community had experienced a surge in tourism once their favorite son rose to the nation's highest office. But unlike Carter, Haley had not maintained a residence in his hometown. Fred Montgomery, a childhood friend of the author and the only black member of the town council, worked closely with state officials to organize the day's festivities, reaching out to local businesses for donations and to residents who were willing to volunteer. People's Bank, the town's sole financial institution, distributed a three-panel pamphlet with the headline splashed on the front page, "A Town on the Upswing," featuring caricatures of both Hickman and Haley. Shops along Main Street began ordering key chains inscribed with "Roots" and "Alex Haley." An eighty-two-year-old African American woman who attended the same church as Alex's family called the impending celebration the "biggest day Henning has ever had."

But resistance persisted from the town's more conservative residents. The mayor advocated a celebration for Jim Hickman, not Haley. Fred Montgomery was undeterred. Active in his church as well as his town, he was often seen as the representative for the black voice in Henning, or as an elderly white woman put it, "the number one colored man in this town." As the event drew closer to its big day, he began receiving threatening phone calls.

On the eve of Tennessee's statewide "Alex Haley Weekend," the police set up alternative traffic routes to Henning to accommodate the expected ten thousand visitors. Local supporters had done their best to beautify the small town; buildings had been painted and the church where Haley's family had gone, as well as the African American cemetery, had gotten makeovers. The house in which he had spent his childhood boasted a welcoming sign, "Henning is the home of Alex Haley."

As the motorcade neared, a news helicopter hovered. Other media began setting up their equipment. Main Street was taken over by orange traffic cones to allow the author, the governor, and the rest of the entourage to make their grand entrance. They were on a tight schedule—something Haley was used to. The band began marching down Main Street with the guest of honor behind it.

Despite fears of racial unrest, the day went without incident. Haley spoke, shook hands, and then was "whisked away." The long-awaited homecoming lasted only four hours. Before the locals could take it all in, he was gone. One angry resident complained she'd hardly even gotten a look at him. "They rushed him in and rushed him out, pushed the poor man from one place to another. I think the politicians have got hold of this thing, and they're milking it for all it's worth."

In the end, there was no renewed economic vitality. The ten thousand anticipated visitors didn't show up; official estimates were closer to one thousand.

The remainder of the three-day, six-city celebration garnered mixed results. A city plagued with a racist past, Memphis's turnout was even more anemic. The city's mayor remained seated behind his office desk for the duration of his brief meeting with Haley. Few showed up at the paltry reception. It wasn't until Haley flew to Knoxville that he was welcomed with open arms. He found a similar welcome in Nashville, speaking before a crowd of ten thousand at Tennessee State University. "Young mothers," a reporter observed, "helped their infant children to get a glimpse of him; and young fathers pointed him out to their sons as he walked by." The wife of a college president, having given her husband photographs of the author, reminded him that if he "did not get those pictures autographed by Mr. Haley, he had better not come home!"

By the end of May, Haley was off to upstate New York to speak at the commencement ceremony at Hamilton College where he had once taught. "Haley Comes Back to Hamilton Roots," read the headline of the local newspaper. The author had fond memories of the small liberal arts school in Clinton, New York. It had offered him an opportunity to escape the fast-paced New York City lifestyle following his successful publication of *The Autobiography of Malcolm X*. Teaching at the college had provided him a steady job, something he hadn't experienced since his service in the US Coast Guard. An adjunct professor, he had been the school's most popular teacher. Stories of Malcolm X's visits to Haley's Greenwich Village basement apartment, the author's time at *Playboy*, and tales of researching his family's history were all soaked up by his predominantly white, upper-class students. As the only African American instructor on campus, he was the ideal candidate to serve as the faculty advisor for the newly formed Black and Puerto Rican Student Union. The most memorable moment of his tenure at Hamilton was when he brought in a *Playboy* bunny, who was a pre-med student, for a Q&A session. Haley's colleagues did not appreciate his unorthodox teaching methods. He never gave tests, rarely took attendance, and often missed class without notice.

Returning to Hamilton, Haley was no longer the hip black man walking around campus with a leather briefcase. Nor was it possible for him to stroll peacefully around the college or visit his favorite doughnut shop in town without being stopped for an autograph. Ebou Manga, the African student who had accompanied Haley on his first trip to Gambia, was astonished by the attention lavished upon the author. Haley seemed used to it.

On a beautiful, sunny afternoon, the commencement ceremony on the campus green was one of the largest attended in the school's hundred-and-fifty-year history. Nearly all the seats were taken and many students (not included in the graduation) sat in the dormitory windows above. The former adjunct professor was introduced as "one of the most famous men in America." Haley had received several honorary degrees over the years, but the one at Hamilton, he often said, meant the most.

Soon after, he was granted the prestigious Southern Christian Leadership Conference's Rosa Parks Award and was asked by the United Negro College Fund to serve as national vice-chairman of its annual campaign. His books continued to sell and his popularity remained undiminished. Anxious to cash in on Rootsmania, Doubleday financed an overseas tour for its star author. By the onset of the summer 1977—nine months since the book's publication and six months since the broadcast—the foreign rights of Roots had been sold, translated, and distributed in nearly all of Western Europe, much of Asia, the Middle East, parts of Africa, and South America. As long as Haley made appearances, the book was expected to exceed sales expectations, and in many countries it did, along with other unanticipated consequences.

Officials in South Africa, for example, feared that the book's release would disrupt their policy of apartheid. On the other side of the Atlantic, in the Bahamas, Roots was being used to rally support against the white candidate during a presidential campaign.

But these were isolated events overshadowed by Haley's enthusiastic audiences. Israelis, who especially took pride in their own roots, warmly welcomed the author. Haley was showered with awards, met Prime Minister Menachem Begin, toured ancient ruins, and lectured at Hebrew University where students were forced to sit in the aisles and stand along the walls.

The most memorable moment of his overseas tour was in Paris. "Alex Haley!" a group of white tourists hollered in thick Kentucky accents from their bus. Haley paused in his tracks as the bus pulled over. Inspired by *Roots,* these Southerners with French ancestry had traveled overseas to "dig up their records." Haley obligingly signed their books.

5

DODGED A BULLET

At the end of the summer, Haley returned to the United States for more book signings, interviews, and lectures. Work dominated his life. Family was a distant second. It was so distant that few knew Haley had ever been married, let alone was a father.

His first wife, Nan Branch, had married him against her father's wishes when she was seventeen and Haley was twenty-one. They soon had two children, Lydia and William. Life together started off well, but due to their ages, lack of real-life experiences, Haley's infidelities, and frequent departures at sea, their relationship quickly went awry. Haley's various mistresses had the audacity, Branch recalled, to "come and ring the bell [at their apartment]." In 1959, when Haley was ready to retire from the coast guard, the couple divorced.

Four years later, while living in the Village, the up-and-coming writer met his second wife, Juliette Collins. They had a daughter, Cynthia, and relocated upstate where he was teaching at Hamilton College. When that relationship failed, he vowed not to remarry.

When Myran "My" Lewis entered Haley's life, he was living in Jamaica working on the *Roots* manuscript. A recent PhD graduate, Lewis' studies had focused on African American culture, including a MA thesis on Malcolm X. She begged Haley to include her in his decade-long project. Twenty-five years his junior, Lewis became more and more involved with Haley's research, writing, and his life. She was initially introduced to friends (never family) as his "editorial assistant" even though they were in the midst of a passionate affair. But once *Roots* hit bookshelves, Lewis was relegated to the background, rarely accompanying him in public. Following his secret wedding to Lewis (Haley had only invited his attorney, Lou Blau, to the ceremony; his brothers weren't even notified), Haley had excused himself and spent the latter part of his wedding night with another woman. Sleeping with multiple women, Haley told childhood friend Fred Montgomery, was something he "couldn't control." And no one was going to tell him what to do.

By late August 1977, Doubleday and Haley came to an undisclosed agreement. Whether it was Haley dropping the suit or Doubleday caving to their best-selling author's demands is not known. One thing was certain. Haley's relationship with his publisher had been irreversibly weakened.

By early fall, Walker's trial was underway. Once again Haley's questionable research methods were scrutinized. Haley's chief researcher and childhood friend, George Sims, had no training and no college degree. Reading the transcript of Sims' and Haley's testimony, Walker concluded that neither man knew how to conduct professional, scholarly research.

Another of Haley's longtime friends, C. Eric Lincoln, who held a PhD and was a well-regarded writer in the field of African American studies, concurred. Knowing Haley, Lincoln had an idea of what transpired. "George [Sims] went into the library and found the facts that Alex needed. . . . [and then] brought back a stack of data and put it in front of Alex and Alex used it, having no sense of the necessity of documentation." To them, it was all fair game.

What mystified Walker was how Doubleday could have allowed a "nonfiction" book to be given a free pass without standard scrutiny or footnotes. Haley always stood by his "faction" definition—the book was both fact and fiction. But what particularly angered Walker was the discovery that Haley hadn't written the book alone. When he began *Roots*, Haley assumed his editor at *Playboy*, Murray Fisher (who had helped edit free of charge *The Autobiography of Malcolm X*) would lend a helping hand, though this time for a considerable fee. But when it came to *Roots*, Fisher's role was more a coauthor than editorial guide. The project consumed so much of his time that Fisher eventually left *Playboy* to concentrate on it, and he'd asked that his name be included on the cover page beneath Haley's.

The more Walker heard about Fisher, who also happened to be white, the more disturbed she became. But Walker made a tactical error by not attending the daily proceedings (her husband was ill), thus making herself unavailable to testify.

The judge ruled that the similarities Walker contested were, at best, "subject to public domain, since it had to do with 'historical or contemporary fact.'" Walker's attorney should have pushed for her to address the court, he added, and her legal counsel had "deviated more often than they should from fundamental rules of evidence and procedure," resulting in "numerous" violations of the court. The case was over. Haley won.

Despite the fallout with Doubleday and the unflattering revelations disclosed during the Walker trial, Haley seemed untouchable. The sequel to *Roots* was underway; the story would begin in the post-Reconstruction era. Haley used a tape recorder to provide details about the latter half of his family history, beginning with his grandmother's childhood. Those recordings were then given to one of the screenwriters from the original miniseries, Ernest Kinoy, to create a three hundred and fifty-page script for *Roots: The Next Generation.*

With two trials down and one to go, Haley must have felt confident about going up against Courlander. The trial would be held in November 1978. The $16 million *Roots* TV sequel was scheduled to air in three months' time. If the trial dragged out or, worse, rendered a guilty verdict, it could impact everything from the sequel's ratings and book sales to funding for Ethnic Studies departments, Gambia's tourism industry, and anything else associated with *Roots*.

6

THE TRIAL

As the trial date approached, Courlander received a stack of what he described as "nasty letters," which he did not disclose to his family. On the other hand, a note of encouragement came from social activist and civil rights organizer Bayard Rustin, who wrote: "If you think you have a solid legal case against Alex Haley, you should proceed regardless of those who assert that a case will damage black pride." And there was good news from his publisher. Bantam was planning to rerelease *The African*; it had been out of print for several years. There was talk of running magazine ads, touting it as "the book that came before the *Roots* experience."

The man who would decide the case was Federal Judge Robert J. Ward. "Courlander vs. Haley" would be Judge Ward's first trial covered by the national media. The press did its best to focus on the core issue at stake: plagiarism. But some black community leaders didn't care whether or not *Roots* had been copied; the point was that slavery and racism had finally been acknowledged. A few went as far to suggest that the case was just another example of whites trying to hold back a black man. Courlander insisted his suit was strictly about "literary justice."

Haley, for his part, maintained that it was inevitable that a successful author would have to endure "such tests as these." As with *Jubilee*, Haley denied having read or even been aware of *The African* prior to the suit against him. The plaintiff, he contended, was just another envious author trying to cash in on his success.

Two Columbia University English professors, Michael Wood and Robert W. Hanning, had been hired to analyze *Roots* and *The African* to determine if any copying had taken place. Their report strengthened Courlander's argument. "The similarities between the two books are not accidental," Hanning wrote. "Without the materials Haley copied from *The African*, *Roots* would have been a far different and, in my opinion, a less effective novel. I believe the materials Haley copied . . . were crucial to the success that *Roots* has achieved."

More telling were the sentiments Judge Ward expressed during the course of the trial. Even before reading the legal briefs, Ward explained, he had read *The African* and *Roots*. Unlike the experts, who analyzed the books, line-by-line, side-by-side, Ward took an "average reader" approach, reading one and then the other. He came to the same con-clusion as the experts.

After three days of testimony, it was time for Haley to take the stand.

"When did you first hear of *The African?*" Courlan-der's attorney asked.

"In the spring of 1977, in connection with an article which appeared in the *New York Times.*" The author was so soft spoken that the court typist asked him if he could speak louder.

"Had you read the book, *The African,* prior to the publication of *Roots?*"

"I had not."

Herb Boyd, who previously had come to Haley's defense, found his response implausible. To have missed either *Jubilee* or *The African,* in Boyd's view, was "almost akin to someone doing a book on the history of the black church in America and knowing nothing of [African American scholar, writer, and activist] W.E.B. Du Bois."

Judge Ward also refused to believe how Haley could have spent more than a decade researching a book about Africans and African Americans without coming across *The African.* The book had been released in the middle of his *Roots* research and had been highly praised by those in the discipline. After hearing the defendant's explanation of his unorthodox research methodology during the trial, Ward expressed his view to the court:

Mr. Haley . . . as I see it, got hold of the book or substantial portions of it . . . made a lot of notes on cards or pieces of papers, shoved them in different folders on subject matter, and then took bits and pieces and worked them in, plugged them into the different subjects that he was addressing in his much longer book.

The general consensus in the courtroom was that Haley had plagiarized *Roots* from *The African*, and had lied about it under oath.

A denial plan, crafted by the writer's defense team, wasn't working anymore. The evidence Haley had been forced to provide the plaintiff prior to the trial demonstrated that he had copied from other books as well, including Shirley Graham's *The Story of Phillis Wheatly*. None of the verbatim passages he copied into his notebooks cited an author's name. Ward's theory seemed right—Haley's way of procuring research material was to either photocopy the document or copy it by hand into one of his many notebooks. It was as if, by inserting these texts into his own binders, they became, miraculously, his own. Courlander, who had written more than twenty books, was taken aback. He had just exposed the most celebrated author of the era as a fraud.

Before the conclusion of the trial, Haley had tried to settle out of court with Courlander for $250,000 (the equivalent today of $1 million). Though it was a substantial sum for Courlander, who was never able to rely on his own royalties to earn a living, he had rejected the offer. Nearly a third of *Roots* came from his own book, he argued. Without

The African, *Roots* would not be *Roots*. At this point, a verdict of guilty seemed inevitable. But Ward knew those following the case, especially in the black community, were going to perceive the proceedings differently, regardless of the evidence and testimony. The judge encouraged the defendant to settle, but Haley would have to propose a more generous amount the second time around. With an estimated net worth of $7.5 million, Haley could afford to offer more, and Courlander knew it. As the trial wound down to its final days, Haley conferred with his attorneys, who were, according to one reporter, reluctant to settle. The day before the verdict was to be rendered, Haley agreed to pay Courlander $650,000 (nearly triple his original offer) and sign a release stating that there were "various" (not eighty-one, as the plaintiff contested) passages from *The African* that had somehow found their way into *Roots*. Courlander was granted a sum of money larger than all of his past earnings from books combined. The trial was over and the racial repercussions feared by Judge Ward did not materialize. And Haley narrowly escaped a reputation-destroying verdict; he didn't even have to acknowledge authorship of the disputed passages in future editions of the book.

With the *Roots* sequel scheduled to air in six weeks, Haley seemed to have regained his equilibrium. Privately, he remained convinced that he was innocent of any wrongdoing. The settlement was not, to his way of thinking, a lucky break. On the contrary, the trial had been unfair and he had been victimized.

Back out on the lecture circuit, determined to satisfy his critics and redeem himself to his fans, Haley presented an arsenal of responses: "The reason for the settlement, at the last minute, was that a skilled lawyer that morning was preparing to paint me as a villain." "How can you explain every word that you write?" "I don't remember where I got something at three a.m. eight years ago." "I became a sitting duck for lawsuits." When asked to elaborate, he didn't hesitate.

Since *Roots* was published in over twenty-five languages and countries, Haley explained, he was vulnerable to suits in each of those jurisdictions. He had to settle.

Besides, he admitted, there was no way he could have accounted for all the information he had accumulated. Out on the road, while writing *Roots*, it wasn't unusual for the author to be given stacks of material by audience members that might be useful in his writing. One of those people had been Native American writer Joseph Bruchac. On Thursday, January 22, 1970, Alex Haley had delivered a lecture at Skidmore College in upstate New York. Bruchac, an ethnic studies instructor at Skidmore, had found Haley "to know so relatively little about" West African history that he'd recommended the then-recently-published historical novel, *The African.* Surprised Haley had not even heard of the book, Bruchac had driven back to his home, three miles away, to retrieve his "own personal copy."

"Here, you can keep it," Bruchac handed the book to Haley. "Thank You," Haley replied, "I'll read it on the plane."

Bruchac was subsequently stunned to read about Courlander's case. He knew his testimony could make a difference. Unfortunately for Courlander, by the time Bruchac decided to write to him, the trial was over.

Almost two years since the original broadcast, *Roots: The Next Generation* aired. Reaching 110 million Americans, it proved to be the second-most watched program in TV history after the initial miniseries. Its higher advertising fees generated more money for Haley than the original. His lecture circuit appearances now paid a minimum of $5,000 per speech. Boosted by the sequel's success, the book's total sales now exceeded eight million copies worldwide.

Although he swore he'd never write again after being emotionally and financially drained from legal battles, the growing list of requests from fellow authors, publishing houses, and periodicals made it difficult for him to abandon his craft. He accepted offers to pen introductions for books about African American history, genealogy, and memoirs of friends. He occasionally wrote an article for *USA Today*'s newspaper insert magazine, *Parade*, and other popular publications. Wealthier than ever, Haley was still beloved by the public. He was, in the words of a *Washington Post* socialite columnist, "now a solid member of the professional class," mingling with both political and Hollywood elite. Among young African Americans, he was voted the "third most admired black man in America . . . after Muhammad Ali and Stevie Wonder."

And to end the decade on a high note, Haley and his brothers purchased their grandparents' home, which they donated to the State of Tennessee. Christened by the Tennessee Historic Landmark Commission as the Palmer House (named after its builder and Haley's beloved grandfather, Will Palmer), it became Tennessee's "first state-owned historic site devoted to African Americans." Located on the newly renamed Haley Avenue, the house was a block away from Hickman Street. Henning had now developed a mini-tourism industry thanks to Alex Haley, not Jim Hickman.

Courlander, meanwhile, published an op-ed in the *Village Voice*. Haley, he wrote, was portraying himself as an "innocent bystander caught in the crush" of his own success. But no one was listening. Courlander would be remembered not for his literary achievements, but for suing the author of *Roots*. According to his son, Michael Courlander, he never got over it.

7

ROOTS UNRAVELED

~~~

By 1980, Haley's two made-for-TV movies had generated tens of millions of dollars. That same year he coproduced *Palmerstown*, a television show, loosely based on his childhood. Formerly the script consultant to *Roots*, Haley's behind-the-camera role had greatly expanded. But the show was cancelled after one and a half seasons.

Though the *Roots* phenomenon began to wane, Haley's presence still inspired jaw-dropping reactions from fans. Always having relished the adoration, the novelty of celebrity nevertheless had worn thin. Speaking to thousands on any given night had become routine. He was almost sixty. It was no longer an adventure to drive 160 miles at four in the morning from Grand Rapids to Detroit on a few hours sleep. Nor to fly from Seattle to Boise then drive to Idaho Falls and leave the next morning for Salt

Lake City, ending the evening with a flight to Columbus, Ohio.

His adoring fans had become more intrusive, asking how much money he made, how much sex he was having, and becoming belligerent if he failed to autograph a book or photograph. Then there were the professional con artists scouting out his fortune. There were constant letters and phone calls from so-called old friends and supposed long-lost relatives demanding handouts. He became less tolerant, less personable, and less friendly.

If the general public could be rude, academics could be ruthless. Two white Southern genealogists from the University of Alabama conducted an analysis of Alex Haley's family as depicted in his book. A husband-and-wife team, Gary and Elizabeth Shown Mills published their findings in the prestigious *Virginia Magazine of History and Biography*. Since they did not have access to Haley's working notes, and *Roots* had neither footnotes nor a reference section, the Mills team was forced to comb through primary source documents from records offices in Maryland, North Carolina, and Virginia. Using what they described as the "most recent guide to genealogical standards" for their benchmark, they discovered that *Roots* failed to meet any of the ten criteria genealogists used to trace lineage. *Roots*, the couple contended, did not meet even the "most basic standards of genealogical inquiry." They found contradictions. They found fabrication. They found inaccuracies in "every pre-Civil War statement of Afro-American lineage in *Roots*." By the end of her research, Elizabeth Mills was convinced that Haley's "mistakes" had been expedient, or, worse, intentional.

Once the Mills' article was out, the media again harassed Haley. He was quick to dismiss the "pious pristine people" who didn't even offer him an opportunity to dispute their findings before publication. Then there was Professor Donald Wright of State University of New York at Courtland. He published similar conclusions in another scholarly journal. An expert in West African oral history, Wright (also white) confirmed Mark Ottaway's earlier assertion that Haley had relied far too heavily on a griot, who was an unreliable source. According to Wright, Haley violated every one of the principles for conducting professional research: Don't make assumptions. Record interviews when possible. Do not provide the answers you are seeking to the interviewee in advance. Do not rely on a single source.

Haley rallied. Those who "come along and say *Roots* was not so . . . [were insinuating] slavery never happened." He promised to address their concerns in his upcoming book, *Search*. Harriet Beecher Stowe had written a similar book more than a century earlier, *The Key to Uncle Tom's Cabin*, following the success of her controversial slave novel. In response to pro-slavery critics, she offered a detailed explanation of the facts behind her story and characters. But Haley's *Search* would never be published.

By 1982, the author was looking to make changes in his life. Although he still spent the majority of his time on the road, his home (where his now-estranged wife, Lewis, con-

tinued to reside) was in Los Angeles. But the fast-pace of
Angelinos did not suit him. That same year the city of
Knoxville was scheduled to host the World's Fair. Haley
accepted an invitation to participate as a celebrated guest.
He was immediately infatuated with the down-to-earth
lifestyle he experienced in Tennessee's third largest city. He
even made a new friend, John Rice Irwin, a white, edu-
cated, eastern-Tennessee native who grew up in the
Appalachian Mountains and was the founder of the
Museum of Appalachia. The two men hit it off, frequently
spending hours discussing history, their love for Tennessee,
and future plans.

Haley purchased a massive farm, a fixer-upper, located
twenty miles north of Knoxville. He was soon the most
popular man in town. Everywhere he went, people, both
black and white, greeted him with smiles and open arms.
The University of Tennessee, Knoxville, even hired him as
a part-time lecturer. He returned the favor, setting up
scholarships at both the university and at nearby schools.
He hired locals to maintain his residence and the 127 acres
of vegetation that surrounded it.

He developed a reputation around town for being generous, and some residents took advantage of it. Haley was
seen as a bit naïve when it came to loaning people money.
He was a millionaire many times over in a region where
that type of wealth was rare. "Everybody was hoping to get
a chunk of his money," according to the spouse of a former
employee of his farm. Those who were close to Haley during these years felt protective of the author, trying to shield

him from the unscrupulous. On one occasion, Haley had confided to his housekeeper that his own children "would never get in touch with him except when they wanted something." He neglected to mention that he'd been far from a model father.

In the mid-to-late 1980s, when he had the time, Haley would escape his still hectic schedule to be at sea. He would travel frequently for weeks or even months, usually by himself. He preferred commercial freight ships that carried only a dozen passengers and crewmembers. Nothing relaxed him more, Haley often said, than being in the middle of the ocean working on a new book or article. In 1988, he published a one-hundred-page novella, *A Different Kind of Christmas*. In comparison to *Roots* and *The Autobiography of Malcolm X*, its sales were unremarkable.

By the end of the decade, Haley had financially "spread himself out too thin." Bad real-estate deals, loans that went unpaid, questionable practices by his financial advisors back in Los Angeles, erratic spending (Haley loved ordering from mail-order catalogs), and slowing sales of *Roots* forced him to liquidate some of his assets in order to stay afloat.

In 1990, at sixty-eight-years-old and in poor health, Haley was now an overweight diabetic who did little to curb his sweet tooth. He still managed to surround himself with a number of girlfriends, in some cases even younger than his estranged wife. Against the wishes of his doctors and close friends, he refused to slow down. His home wasn't in Knoxville, Los Angeles, New York City, or, for that matter, Henning. He was a nomad—ironically, root-less. His life was his writing and his love was lecturing—as long as the touring schedule didn't exceed his limits. A natural orator, there was nowhere else he'd rather be than standing in front of a group of people and telling a story. The size of an audience never mattered, though the audiences were smaller and more intimate now. Fulton Oursler Jr., his former editor at *Reader's Digest*, remembered that Haley could "hypnotize one human being or a crowd of a hundred thousand people."

In early February 1992, Haley left his farm and flew to the West Coast for a series of lectures, endorsement deals, and meetings with Hollywood executives. A few days later, on February 10, while en route to a speaking engagement in Seattle, he suffered a fatal heart attack.

8

A COMPLICATED
LEGACY

The announcement of Haley's death was on the front page
of every daily newspaper in the United States and the lead
story in all the major television news programs. President
George H.W. Bush issued a public statement. The state of
Tennessee was in mourning. Funeral services were held in
Memphis, Henning, Knoxville, and at John Rice Irwin's
museum.

His brother George Haley, serving as the estate's execu-
tor, soon discovered a financial mess. Haley's first wife,
Nan, and his third wife, My, (whom George hadn't even
met) contested the will, as did a number of others, including several mistresses, his friend George Sims, and the
funeral home in Memphis where Haley's ceremony was

held (the bill was never paid). It was assumed Haley had died a rich man; in fact, he died in debt. At one point, he had been one of the wealthiest authors in the country. George, who had served in presidential administrations and was a well-respected Washington, DC lawyer, had no choice but to auction off his brother's assets and anything else that could be used to pay back $1.5 million in outstanding debt. Everything, including unpublished manuscripts, his Pulitzer Prize award, notebooks full of ideas for prospective stories, personal correspondence, television scripts, items from his days in the coast guard, and the original "two cans of sardines and eighteen cents," eventually framed once he became wealthy, was for sale to the highest bidder.

It wasn't long before the court proceedings began to determine who had rights to his future royalties from *Roots* and books expected to be released. It was decided that they would be divided in thirds—Haley's three children, his two brothers, and his third wife, My, would each receive a portion. Following a series of legal encounters with Haley's brother, George, eventually My went bankrupt and had no choice but to sell her hard-fought literary rights for a low sum. His first two wives, Nan and Juliette, as well as friend and researcher George Sims, were allocated a small amount of money.

Soon after the struggles over the estate, Haley's legacy sustained yet another blow by an exposé published in the *Village Voice*. Of all the articles challenging the validity of

Roots, Philip Nobile's "Uncovering Roots" was the most damning.

At the outset, Nobile had experienced reluctance about "going after a legend in the black community." But after conducting research in Alex Haley's papers at the University of Tennessee, Knoxville, Nobile concluded that *Roots* was an outright fraud. His article would later serve as the basis for an inflammatory BBC-sponsored documentary, *The Roots of Alex Haley* (1997), which was aired in the United Kingdom but not in the United States.

It seemed Nobile had all but hammered the final nail in Alex Haley's coffin. Having once sold sixty-seven thousand copies of *Roots* in a single day, the book would—in a decade following his death and in a quarter of a century after its epic broadcast—go out of print.

Still, noticeable traces of book and author remain. In his beloved Knoxville, a 4,200-pound statue of the author sits atop Alex Haley Heritage Square. His 127-acre estate outside of Knoxville, the Haley Farm, was eventually sold to the nonprofit Children's Defense Fund and is used as a retreat center. The Alex Haley Museum and Interpretive Center (originally known as the Palmer House) in Henning is considered one of Tennessee's top tourist attractions. In Annapolis, a statue of Haley rests on the City Dock, serving as the "only monument in the United States commemorating the name and place of arrival of an enslaved African." The US Coast Guard named a 282-foot-long cutter after its most famous member, the first time a military vessel was named after a journalist. On a smaller scale, two college dormitories are named after Haley (one at his father's alma mater, North Carolina A&T State University, and one at Bowie State University), as well as an inner-city charter school in Chicago (Alex Haley Academy), a celebrity golf tournament in Knoxville, and a municipal swimming pool in Ithaca (Haley's birthplace).

With the assistance of writer David Stevens, who used the author's detailed notes and outlines, the estate released two more books under Haley's name, *Queen: The Story of An American Family* (1993) and *Mama Flora's Family* (1999). Both books would eventually be turned into made-for-television movies.

Aside from permanent memorials and publications, occasionally Haley's work and ideas have been acknowledged. Recently, for example, in January 2013, during President Barack Obama's Inauguration on the steps of the United States Capitol, one of the speakers, Haley's longtime friend, Tennessee Senator Lamar Alexander, began his comments: "The late Alex Haley, the author of 'Roots,' lived his life by these six words: 'Find the good and praise it.'"

After thirty-five years, the original *Roots* miniseries still has six of its eight episodes in the category of most-watched programs, including the final episode that ranks as the third most-watched program ever. And the book itself, after a five-year lull, was picked up by a new publisher and reprinted, finding new shelf life in bookstores and online.

Since its publication and broadcast, *Roots* continues to resonate in our modern culture—from television shows devoted to tracing a celebrity's roots to websites that have ignited yet another surge in genealogy. For all that was wrong with *Roots*, the book's impact and its message cannot be denied. "Whatever its flaws," the *New York Times* editorial team wrote two days following Alex Haley's death, "*Roots* opened modern America's eyes to [its] black heritage...its impact was phenomenal."

Author's Note

As a self-published author, reader book reviews on Amazon, GoodReads, iTunes, or Kobo are a critical component of a writer's success. When you have a moment, please take an opportunity to let the reading public know what you thought of *Alex Haley's* Roots.

NOTES

"Did you have any idea?": Alex Haley, "*Roots*, Plus 12 Years; The Ups and Downs of a Successful Author," *Washington Post*, February 12, 1989.

"Your life will never be the same again": Susan King, "The Roots of Change," *Los Angeles Times*, January 19, 1992.

"two cans of sardines and eighteen cents": Joy Wansley and Lois Armstrong, "Alex Haley's Search for *Roots* Took Him First to the Brink of Suicide, and Now to Fame and Riches," *People Weekly*, October 18, 1976.

"unlocked": Alex Haley, *Roots: The Saga of an American Family* (Garden City, NY: Doubleday & Company, 1976), p. 669.

"thrilled to be driving the newly famous writer": Jacqueline Trescott, "Alex Haley: The Author of *Roots*, Astride His Moment of Fame," *Washington Post*, January 28, 1977.

"Hey, brother, that's a magnificent piece of work.": Ibid.

"the most significant civil rights event": James Thomas Jackson, "Awakening to a Common Suffering and Pride," *New York Times*, February 8, 1977.

"drastic drop": Jerry Buck, "Making TV History: Viewers Pulled in by *Roots*," *Los Angles Times*, January 29, 1977.

"Rootsmania": Rhoygnette Ellison, "Rhoygnette's Revelations," *Chicago Metro News*, March 5, 1977.

"Sir": Alex Haley, "There Are Days When I Wish It Hadn't Happened," *Playboy*, March 1979.

"I want to thank you for what you've done for America.": Ibid.

"Alex Haley": Ibid.

"That's him!": Ibid.

"He ain't goin' nowhere!": Alex Haley, "*Roots*, Plus 12 Years."

"Mr. Haley seated at a small table": James H. Brady, "In the Matter of Alex Haley's *Roots*," *Baltimore Sun*, February 6, 1977.

"heavy, courteous and civilized": Terrance O'Flaherty, "TV Today," *San Francisco Chronicle*, February 14, 1977.

"inflame": Robert E Strain, "Alex Haley's 'Roots' – A Family Triumph,"*Los Angeles Times* ("Letters to the *Times*"), February 6, 1977.

"blacks were just getting settled down": "Why *Roots* Hit Home," *Time*, February 14, 1977.

"Haley is one author, who won't end his day in a garret.": "Haley's Quest for Roots," *Forbes*, February 15, 1977.

"Alex Haley, Roots, U.S.A.": Alex Haley, "*Roots*, Plus 12 Years."

"flooded with appeals for help": Marjorie Hyer, "Mormon Microfilmed Roots in Great Demand," *Washington Post*, March 4, 1977.

"most wanted man in the nation": "*Roots*' Haley talks about rags to riches," *Tuenawanda News Frontier*, February 19, 1977.

"Kinte": Hans J. Massquoi, "Alex Haley: The Man Behind *Roots*," *Ebony*, April 1977.

"phony excuse just to go to the bathroom": Linda Witt, "Haley's *Roots*: Stung by Accusations, Alex Haley Returns to the Village Where He Found His *Roots*," *People Weekly*, May 9, 1977.

"national monument": James Pringle, "To the Roots of *Roots*," *Newsweek*, March 14, 1977.

"reporter with a reputation for integrity": Robert D. McFadden, "Some Points of *Roots* questioned; Haley Stands by Book As a Symbol," *New York Times*, April 10, 1977.

“grave flaws”: PHS, *The Times* Diary: Sticking Pins into A Best-Seller,” *The* [London] *Times*, April 12, 1977.

“trading post”: Mark Ottaway, “Tangled Roots,” *The* [London] *Sunday Times*, April 10 1977.

“notorious unreliability”: Ibid.

“playboy”: Ibid.

“doubts about Fofana’s [the griot’s] reliability”: Ibid.

“so confusing, so obscured by contradictory statements from different sources”: Ibid.

“neither you nor I know exactly what happened”: Ibid.

“symbol of the fate of my people.”: Ibid.

“I spent twelve years doing this book.”: PHS, *The Times* Diary: Sticking Pins into A Best-Seller.”

“looking for a headline”: Malcolm R. West, “Black Historians Reflect on Criticism of *Roots*,” *Jet*, April 28, 1977.

“like saying that Anne Frank never existed or that the whole Nazi thing was a hoax”: Kenneth L. Woodward and Anthony Collings, “The Limits of ‘Faction,’” *Newsweek*, April 25, 1977.

“misconstrued”: Tom Zito, “The Gambia and the *Roots* of Tourism,” *Washington Post*, May 17, 1977.

"broader attempt to demean anything Black people have to say about the slavery experience": Malcolm R. West, "Black Historians Reflect on Criticism of *Roots*."

"Mr. Haley to be a man of great integrity": Herb Boyd, "*Roots'* Naw, Rutz, Dummy," *Essence*, August 1977.

"head on": "Haley Defends *Roots* Facts; Author Charges British Reporter Made 'Unfounded Accusations,'" *Washington Post*, April 11, 1977.

"'I'll be damned.'": "Author Haley Reporter Moore Win Pulitzers," *Jet*, May 5, 1977.

"'Aw shit, baby,' he murmured.": Linda Witt, "Haley's Roots: Stung by Accusations."

"numerous similarities": Robert D. McFadden, "Novelist's Suit Charges *Roots* Copied Parts of her 1966 Book," *New York Times*, April 23, 1977.

"ridiculous": Ibid.

"who write blockbuster books": Ibid.

"smacked of bitterness": Jacqueline Trescott, "Respected Scholar; Margaret Walker Has Intense Feelings On Black Writers' Spiritual Alliance," *Washington Post*, April 28, 1977.

"verbatim copying": Christopher Dickey, "*Roots* Author Facing Accusations; Novelist's Suit Charges Haley's Book is 'Largely Copied,'" *Washington Post*, April 28, 1977.

"up against something incalculably great in force": Harold Courlander, "*Roots, The African*, and the Whisky Jug Case," *Village Voice*, April 9, 1979.

"open season": Christopher Dickey, "*Roots* Author Facing Accusations; Novelist's Suit Charges Haley's Book is 'Largely Copied,'"

"more than half the profits of *Roots*": Arnold H. Lubasch, "Suit Says *Roots* Copied from Novel," *New York Times*, November 9, 1978.

"most illustrious son": Othal H. Lakey, "A Day with Alex Haley," *The Christian Index*, June 9, 1977.

"may be the nearest thing": John Egerton, "Homecoming," *New Times*, July 8, 1977, Box 29, Folder 11, John Egerton Papers, Special Collections and University Archives, Vanderbilt University.

"lone policeman and judge": "Roots Effect on Henning, Who Knows," *The Tennessean*, April 18, 1977.

"niggers": John Egerton, "Homecoming."

"biggest day Henning has ever had": Ibid.

"the number one colored man in this town": Ibid.

"whisked away": Ibid.

"They rushed him in and rushed him out.": Ibid.

"Young mothers": Othal H. Lakey, "A Day with Alex Haley."

"did not get those pictures autographed by Mr. Haley": Ibid.

"Haley Comes back to Hamilton Roots": "Haley Comes back to Hamilton Roots," *The* [Utica, NY] *Daily Press*, May 30, 1977.

"one of the most famous men in America": Roy Schecter, "Spotlight: Commencement," *Hamilton Magazine,* Spring 1977, Alexander 'Alex' Haley Folder, Hamilton College Archives.

"dig up their records": Jeffery Elliot, "Alex Haley Talks to Jeffery Elliot," *Negro History Bulletin* (Jan/Feb 1978), pp. 782-785.

"come and ring the bell": Interview of Nan Haley, February 22, 1992 (transcript), Series I, Sub-Series A: Transcripts, 1986-1992, Box 1, Folder 6, Anne Romaine Collection of Alex Haley, MS. 2828, University of Tennessee, Knoxville, Library Special Collections Research Services.

"editorial assistant": Hans J. Massquoi, "Alex Haley: The Man Behind *Roots*."

"couldn't control": Romaine Cassette Interviews of Fred Montgomery, February 23, 1992, Series I, Sub-Series B: Audiotapes, 1986-1992, Box 2, Folder 7, Anne Romaine Collection of Alex Haley, MS. 2828, University of Tennessee, Knoxville, Library Special Collections Research Services.

"George [Sims] went into the library.": Haley Book Interview of Dr. C. Eric Lincoln, undated (transcript), Series I, Subject Files: 1958-1995, Box 3, Folder 14, Anne Romaine Collection, MS. 2032, University of Tennessee, Knoxville, Library Special Collections Research Services.

"nonfiction": Eliot Fremont-Smith, "Alex Haley and Rot in *Roots*," *Village Voice*, May 30, 1979.

"faction": Harold Courlander, "*Roots, The African*, and the Whisky Jug Case."

"subject to public domain": "Alexander vs. Haley: Opinion #4766840," Fulton Oursler, Jr. Papers, Box 2, Folder 6, Georgetown University Library Special Collections Research Center, Washington, D.C.

"deviated more often than they should": Ibid.

"numerous": Ibid.

"nasty letters": Jacqueline Trescott, "Roots of Victory; For Courlander, It's All in 40 Years' Work," *Washington Post*, December 16, 1978.

"if you think you have a solid legal case": Bayard Rustin to Harold Courlander, November 29, 1978, in possession of Michael Courlander.

"the book that came before the *Roots* experience": Christopher Dickey, "*Roots* Author Facing Accusations."

"literary justice": Jacqueline Trescott, "Roots of Victory."

"such tests as these": Christopher Dickey, "*Roots* Author Facing Accusations."

"The similarities between the two books": Robert W. Hanning, "Plantiffs' Pre-Trial Memorandum and Proposed Findings of Fact and Conclusions of Law," Volume III, Report of Professor Robert W. Hanning, Professor of English and Comparative Literature, Columbia University." United States District Court, Southern District of New York (1978), 77 Civ. 2546 (RJW) p.1.

"average reader": "Harold Courlander v. Alex Haley, 1978" United States District Court, Southern District of New York (1978) p.1295

"When did you first hear of *The African?*": Ibid., p.1386

"In the spring of 1977": Ibid., pp.1386-1387

"almost akin to someone doing a book": Herb Boyd, "Plagiarism and the *Roots* Suits," *First World: An International Journal of Black Thought*, 2 (1979) p.32

"Mr. Haley as I see it": "Harold Courlander v. Alex Haley, 1978" United States District Court, Southern District of New York (1978) p.1309 "various": Phil Stanford, "Roots and Grafts on the Haley Story," *The Washington Star*, April 8, 1979.

"The reason for the settlement": Mary Seibert McCauley, "Alex Haley, A Southern Griot: A Literary Biography," p. 199, Ph.D. Dissertation, Vanderbilt University, 1983

"How can you explain every word that you write?": Ibid.

"I don't remember.": Jan Herman (*Chicago Sun-Times News Service*),"Haley's Life 'Is a Blur' After Plagiarism Settlement," *The* [Memphis] *Commercial Appeal*,December 30, 1978.

"I became a sitting duck for lawsuits.": Alex Haley, "There Are Days When I Wish It Hadn't Happened."

"to know so relatively little about": Joseph Bruchac to Harold Courlander, December 15, 1978, in possession of Michael Courlander.

"him my own personal copy": Ibid.

"Here, you can keep it.": Phil Sanford, "*Roots* and Grafts," *Inquiry*, April 16, 1979.

"now a solid member of the professional class": Joseph McLellan,"The Return of *Roots*: A Preview with the Haley Family," *Washington Post*, January 15, 1979.

"third most admired black man in America": Richard M. Levine, "*Roots* and Branches," *New Times*, September 4, 1978.

"first state-owned historic site": Carol Van West, "Alex Haley State Historic Site,"*The Tennessee Encyclopedia of History and Culture,* Version 2.0, January 1, 2010. http://tennesseeencyclopedia.net/entry.php?rec=587

"innocent bystander": Harold Courlander, "*Roots, The African,* and the Whisky Jug Case."

"most recent guide to genealogical standards": Gary B. Mills and Elizabeth Shown Mills, "*Roots* and the New 'Faction:' A Legitimate Tool for Clio?," *Virginia Magazine of History and Biography,* 89 (January 1981), p.7.

"most basic standards of genealogical inquiry": Ibid., p.24.

"every pre-Civil War statement of Afro-American lineage in *Roots*": Ibid., p.6.

"mistakes": James Kent, director, "The Roots of Alex Haley," *BBC Documentary,* 1997.

"pious pristine people": Mary Seibert McCauley, "Alex Haley, A Southern Griot: A Literary Biography," p.183.

"come along and say *Roots* was not so": Ibid.

"Everybody was hoping to get a chunk of his money.": Author's interview of Girdie King and her husband, May 21, 2010

"would never get in touch with him": Ibid.

"spread himself out too thin": Ibid.

"hypnotize one human being": Author's interview of Fulton Oursler, Jr., September 6, 2010.

"going after a legend in the black community": James Kent, "The Roots of Alex Haley."

"only monument in the United States": Nelson Hernandez, "A Symbol of History and Hope," *Washington Post*, June 13, 2002.

"The late Alex Haley, the author of 'Roots,'": Rachel Weiner, "Why Lamar Alexander Quoted Alex Haley" *Washington Post*, January 21, 2013

"Whatever its flaws": Editorial, *New York Times*, February 12, 1992.

My Journey

Writing a book is no longer a dream but a reality, if you have an editor, cover designer, and a marketing plan in tow. Today, self-published writers like myself have the freedom to choose the book cover, hire the editor, determine the length of the book, how it will be promoted, when it will be published, and how much the book will cost.

The publishing industry is different than a decade ago. With the advent of Amazon Kindle Digital Publishing and a cadre of other do-it-yourself publishing resources available online, the book business is entering terrain that no one ever could have predicted. What was once looked down upon, self-publishing has now become a legitimate and viable opportunity for neophyte and veteran writers alike.

Every self-published author has his or her story of how they made the decision to bypass traditional channels and go out on their own.

Through a series of published blogs, here's my story.

A SEED HAD BEEN PLANTED

November 19, 2013

http://adamhenig.com/2013/11/19/matt-olmstead/

Unless you've worked on the set of the 1990s hit ABC television series *NYPD Blue* (or are obsessed with Fox's *Prison Break* or A&E's *Breakout Kings*), odds are you're not familiar with Matt Olmstead.

In 1988, Matt Olmstead graduated from California State University, Chico, (or better known as Chico State) a school that, regrettably, is more known for its partying than its academics. I ought to know, having attended the university a decade later.

In 2001, when I was a junior, majoring in political science and aspiring to become a lawyer, Chico State honored Olmstead with the Distinguished Alumnus Award for his career as an accomplished screenwriter in Hollywood. He's best known for his work on *NYPD Blue*.

Given Olmstead's achievements, most universities also would have honored him. But at Chico, where professors often characterize the school as a training center for teachers and mid-level managers, Olmstead was a diamond in the rough. It was rare for Chico State to have a graduate who succeeded in Hollywood, even if it was behind the camera.

One day, while I was standing in the hallway with classmates, waiting for my professor to arrive, I noticed a flyer on the bulletin board. It announced a free event that evening featuring Olmstead.

Having been a *NYPD Blue* fan, I took the flyer from the board and planned on attending. Expecting it to be poorly attended—it was tough to compete against "buck night" at the bars—I was shocked to find there was not an empty seat. People were either standing in the back or sitting on the carpet at the front of the room. I opted for the floor.

What made this guest lecturer different than others in the past?

Matt Olmstead was not just another high-priced speaker. Chico State had sponsored plenty of those lecturers (e.g., writer Maya Angelou, musician Henry Rollins, and former Israeli Prime Minister Shimon Peres). In the doting eyes of this audience, he was one of us!

No podium or lectern, Olmstead kept it informal. His premise was to focus on how he got to where he did and, conversely, why being a writer was not as glamorous as one might envision, even in Hollywood.

The number one mistake most aspiring writers make, he pointed out, was wasting a huge amount of time. Olmstead spent his first months in Los Angeles, for example, wearing black turtlenecks and smoking cigarettes all day at a street café while sharing ideas with fellow writers. Once he figured out he was going nowhere, he quit smoking and put away the turtlenecks. Over the next few years, while working odd jobs to help pay his rent, Olmstead made time to hone his craft. Like all writers, rewriting was what he spent the majority of his time doing.

Though he cloistered himself in his apartment, away from the beautiful beaches and the Sunset Strip, there were hardly any guarantees. Determined to make a living as a full-time writer, Olmstead persevered. Ultimately, through hard work, cultivating relationships within the industry, and a little bit of luck, he landed a job at ABC.

I had never thought of writing as a career for myself, but after that evening, the seed had been planted. I still focused on law (although that would eventually go by the wayside), but writing always remained within reach. I kept a journal, crafted short stories, and even penned a couple of unfinished screenplays.

Eventually, I found my niche, biography, and my subject, Alex Haley.

WE LEFT OUR HEART IN KNOXVILLE

February 14, 2014
http://insideofknoxville.com/2014/02/we-left-our-heart-in-knoxville/
Originally published by InsideofKnoxville.com

It was my first trip to Tennessee.

Hell, aside from Austin and Miami, it was my first experience in the South.

Traveling from the bluest of blue states, California, where Obama and Planned Parenthood bumper stickers are proudly displayed, my girlfriend (soon-to-be wife) Jennifer and I were in for a bit of culture shock when we arrived in Knoxville.

"What brings you here," was the most frequent question we were asked during our brief stay. Locals were dumbfounded why two West Coasters would make the trek to the Eastern part of the Volunteer State.

Two words (and it wasn't the Smoky Mountains).

"Alex Haley."

Immediately, we were told to go to the Alex Haley Square. I was planning to visit the site, but my purpose was to conduct research in order to write the first biography about the author of *Roots*. Although his personal papers are under lock and key, Haley's designated biographer (who died before completing the project), Anne Romaine, made her research open to the public. Her manuscripts and related materials are so vast and vital to anyone wanting to reconstruct Haley's life, visiting Knoxville is a must.

Since I didn't have an agent or a publisher, I was covering the entire cost for the two plane tickets, five nights in a downtown hotel, meals, and incidentals.

"So, we travelled all the way to Knoxville to go to a library," Jennifer continued to inquire in the taxi en route to our hotel. "That seems so strange."

"Don't worry, we'll go out to dinner and there will be time to shop."

A smile emerged, but just a little one.

The first two days in Knoxville were spent at the university's library. We arrived when the Special Collections division opened and stayed until we were asked to leave. Our lunch consisted of a bagel, yogurt, a banana and coffee at the library's in-house Starbucks–of course, we couldn't take any of the goodies inside. Jennifer helped out with making copies, which numbered in the hundreds, and kept the files and folders organized to the staff's delight.

On the third and final full day of research, I cut it short so we could explore the city's downtown. We walked over to Market Square to find it bustling with outdoor dining venues, live music, sidewalk vendors, and couples and families mulling about, enjoying the temperate weather. Jennifer and I were taken aback.

Which European city were we in? Was this really Knoxville?

With her shopping radar on, Jennifer immediately zeroed in on Bliss, a chic fashion boutique. She was in heaven.

An hour later, we ate delicious pizza at Tomato Head. From there, we walked along Gay Street, admiring the architecture, the Knoxville Theater marquee, and, eventually, the waterfront.

I admit I had preconceived stereotypes of what life was like in Knoxville. This was not what I had expected.

The next day, we rented a car, stopped by Alex Haley Square (and, of course, took a picture), and then drove north to visit John Rice Irwin's Museum of Appalachia. On our way back, we stopped off in the older section of town. Surrounded by railroad tracks and a series of abandoned buildings, we stumbled upon a pub, a tattoo parlor, and a used record store, the capstone to any hip town.

Now, I was in heaven!

That evening we walked down Gay Street, toward the waterfront, and ate at The Bistro. Our friendly and inquisitive waiter (who not surprisingly asked, "What brings you to Knoxville?"), provided us with two complimentary tickets to a bluegrass show at the Bijou Theater, which was next door. The show was entertaining and on our jaunt back to the hotel, we wandered through World's Fair Park.

Relaxing along the river that runs through the park, with the signature golden golf ball (leftover from the 1982 World's Fair) staring down upon us, Jennifer, cradled in my arms, whispered to me.

"I could live here."

I agreed.

Although reality sunk in once we returned to the Bay Area, our fondness for the Prismatic City remained.

ANNE ROMAINE, ALEX HALEY'S FIRST BIOGRAPHER

January 25, 2014
http://adamhenig.com/2014/01/25/718/

To his colleagues and friends, it was a bit of a shock—Alex Haley hired a white, southern folk singer to serve as his official biographer. It was the mid-1980s, less than a decade after publication of *Roots*. Haley, in his early sixties, was still a household name and remained one of America's most popular literary figures. With access to the best-known writers, why would the Pulitzer Prize-winning author select a singer to pen his life story?

Those close to him were perplexed. Was Haley using Romaine to shake off other potential biographers, who would likely uncover the many skeletons in his closet? Did she have the skills to write such a book? Even if she did, would she even complete it?

Although Romaine had been cast as a backwoods musician and political radical, she was not without credentials. Twenty-two years younger than her subject, Romaine earned her master's from the University of Virginia and eventually worked as a curator at the Alex Haley Museum in the early 1980s. Not surprisingly, it was where the two met.

Romaine expressed an interest in writing Haley's life story. The author consented, providing Romaine access to his papers and agreeing to be interviewed. He notified family members, friends, and associates to make themselves available too.

The quirky yet relentless, often unprepared but passionate Anne Romaine spent the next decade ignoring criticism and did what any good biographer does—gather as much information about her subject's life and never take no for an answer.

Whether it was a best-selling writer, an Oscar-winning actor, or a lowly, retired Coast Guardsman, Romaine was determined to speak to anyone who ever associated with Haley. She met, interviewed, and recorded (and, in many cases, transcribed) nearly a hundred interviews.

Unfortunately, Romaine should have consulted other biographers prior to starting the project. Having been versed in the craft, she would have avoided unnecessary mistakes.

In 1989, for instance, Romaine interviewed Malcolm X's widow, Betty Shabazz. During the course of the one-hour interview, Shabazz was clearly annoyed when Romaine raised questions about her late husband, questions which had little relevance to Haley.

In trying to characterize Haley's and Malcolm X's relationship (when they were at work on the *Autobiography of Malcolm X*) as "father and son," it was Shabazz who pointed out to Romaine that Haley was only four years older than her husband, hardly enough of an age difference to justify that description.

On another occasion, in her interview with Haley's former editor at *Playboy*, Murray Fisher, the would-be biographer began asking questions about his background. The interviewee was annoyed. Not one to mince words, Fisher, an experienced interviewer, reminded Romaine that all of her questions thus far could easily have been answered by reading the resume that he had sent her in advance.

Not able to regain her composure, Romaine stumbled over the remaining questions. In fact, oddly, it was Fisher who took over the interview and began asking Romaine what she found out about his old friend.

When Romaine interviewed Haley's former staffers, she spent the majority of the session asking about their own lives and not much about their former employer. In one interview, for example, Romaine failed to take into consideration the impact of the location, which was a noisy diner. Since Romaine recorded all of her interviews with a hand-held device, the outside clamor was easily picked up, making it difficult to understand what was being said.

And yet, despite her flaws, Romaine was quite effective. Determined to fulfill the task at hand, she met with nearly everyone who had ever associated with the author–his brothers, half-sister, son, eldest daughter, one of his ex-wives, his childhood friends, the editors of *Roots*, fellow writers, and those affiliated with the *Roots* movie, no one was off limits.

Tenacious as ever, she also unearthed secrets about her subject.

One of Romaine's most interesting and insightful sessions was with Haley's younger brother, former Kansas State Senator and Ambassador to the Gambia, George Haley.

Having already met on prior occasions, Romaine and George had cultivated a relatively warm relationship. The interview took place almost one year after Alex Haley had died. Speaking on the phone, the two spent a considerable time analyzing Alex's faults as husband and father.

George revealed that Alex considered him, in view of his solid marriage and relationship with his children, to be the "fortunate" one of the family.

As Romaine became seasoned as an interviewer, she continued to amass fascinating nuggets of information about her subjects.

In the end, however, Romaine never wrote the book. She died in 1995, three years after Haley.

But her efforts were not in vain. All of the recorded interviews are stored away and available to the public in the Anne Romaine Papers at the University of Tennessee, Knoxville, library's special collections division. Romaine's recordings and transcripts as well as the thousands of pages of documents she accumulated over the decade-long project remains to this day the most important assemblage of material about the author of *Roots*.

THE MAN FROM APPALACHIA

May 31, 2014
https://medium.com/@adamhenig/the-man-from-appalachia-9881a994196c

One day. That's all we had.

Jennifer understood that this was supposed to be a business trip. Flying to Knoxville, Tennessee, from San Francisco, California, along with hotel accommodations, was necessary in order to complete my biography of Alex Haley.

Setting aside a week, two days for flying, left us five full days to conduct research at the University of Tennessee,

Knoxville, main library's special collections division. Since we were planning to spend every minute in the library, literally from opening to closing, we decided to allocate one day for non-research.

We had already explored Knoxville's lively downtown. In the eastern part of the Volunteer State, there were two main attractions—the Smokey Mountains and Dollywood, Dolly Parton's own amusement park. Both were more than an hour's drive away and I would have preferred not to spend so much time on the road.

After consulting our guidebook, we opted for the Museum of Appalachia. Located about 15 miles north of Knoxville, we rented a car and started our journey.

Thanks to a large billboard advertising the Museum's exit along the highway, we arrived at our destination, which upon initial view looked more like a farm.

Once we paid the admission and walked through the gift shop, we took a self-guided tour of the Appalachian Hall of Fame. Located in a barn, the Hall of Fame was an exhibit hall that featured thousands of artifacts associated with Appalachia. From hand tools and cooking ware to musical instruments and children's toys, the items on display conveyed what life was like in nineteenth and early twentieth century Appalachia.

There was information about Appalachians who grew up to become popular figures such as Texas Senator and Governor Sam Houston, World War I hero Sgt. Alvin York, and FDR's Secretary of State Cordell Hull. They even had photographs of famous museum visitors including, to my delight, Alex Haley.

Afterwards, along the grounds, we explored the various log cabins that encircled the farm. One cabin had banjo music blaring from it. It was a trio of bluegrass musicians performing for two other visitors before we entered. They played as if there were a hundred people inside. I don't think more than six could fit.

After their set was finished, one of the band members asked where we were from. She was astonished to learn that we came as far away as California—apparently it was rare to encounter visitors who travelled beyond the surrounding states.

"What are y'all doin' here?" she inquired in her southern accent.

"I'm writing a book about Alex Haley," I responded.

"Well, y'know who owns this place, right?"

"No," I replied.

"John Rice Irwin."

"Who?"

Born and raised during the Great Depression, from the moment he could walk and talk, John Rice Irwin seemed destined to make Appalachian culture a part of his life. With Southern Appalachian roots traced back to the 1700's, John took pride in his ancestry. In fact, his grandfather noticed at an early age how his grandson gravitated toward the family's heritage, wanting to collect and preserve as many items as possible.

"[You] ought to start a little museum of these old-timey things some time," he told his grandson.

And so Irwin did.

It began at a public auction in the early 1960s with the purchase of a nineteenth century horseshoe box for $4. After acquiring a few more items, the collector finally made his first big purchase—a decrepit, one-room log cabin. That was the beginning. Irwin would set out to acquire as many items related to Appalachia as he possibly could. With two acres of land and a log cabin, the museum would expand in size and depth beyond the founder's wildest dreams.

Over the next two decades, Irwin's property grew to sixty-five acres complete with over two-dozen Appalachia-style structures that included a schoolhouse, a 19th century jail cell, and the "Dan'l Boone Cabin" used on the set of a 1950s television show about the frontiersman. Eventually, the museum had become one of the most popular attractions in the state. In 2007, it was declared by the Smithsonian Institution as one of its Affiliate members, a prestigious honor.

"John Rice Irwin is the founder of this place," the banjo player went on. "And he knew Alex Haley. They were tight. I bet you he's here...in that office of his."

I was shocked. Here we were, supposed to spend the day not conducting research. I turned to Jennifer. I felt guilty that we were still focusing on Alex Haley. As always, she was a good sport, and knew the importance of meeting Mr. Irwin.

"He's not as active as he used to be. He sorta looks like Mark Twain but without the mustache."

We made the trek back to the museum entrance. I walked over to the gift shop clerk and asked to speak to Mr. Irwin.

"And what is this pertaining to?" she eyed me with a bit of suspicion.

For a moment, I was unsure what to say. I was nervous. It wasn't my first interview—I had managed to conduct two earlier in the week with members of the library staff who were acquaintances of Haley—but this was different. If Haley and Irwin were as close as the musician said they were, I knew it was vital for my book.

"One moment," she responded, after I told her I was a biographer of Alex Haley. She wandered off to a backdoor.

Within three minutes, she returned.

"Okay, honey, he'll see you. Just go through that door [she pointed] and turn left."

I grabbed Jen and off we went to meet the man from Appalachia.

The cigar smoke permeated the back area. Through a storage room, we were led into a conference room with a half-dozen five-foot high file cabinets up against the walls. This was not something you saw much anymore—endless amounts of papers filed away. It easily could have been part of the exhibit too. But it wasn't, not exactly. It was Mr. Irwin's personal papers. Like any good curator, he kept records of everything.

From there, we wandered into Mr. Irwin's office. Sitting

behind a desk, dangling an unlit cigar from his lips was the man from Appalachia.

He stared at me, wanting to know my business. Was I a reporter? Was this a hit piece on his old friend? It had been years since anyone was interested in Alex Haley.

"Take a seat," he mumbled but remained grim. He did resemble Mark Twain—wild white hair, thick eyebrows, and a stern gaze—but without the signature mustache.

No longer young and energetic, Mr. Irwin was eighty-years-old. His role at the museum was mostly ceremonial. He leaned back in his chair. As I scanned the contents of his office, it was as if time had stood still. There was nothing displayed that showed we were living in the 21st century. He was certainly stuck in the past. He had become, strangely, part of the museum too.

"What can I do for you?" his voice rose a little louder and clearer.

I began explaining the biography I was writing about Alex Haley and how I ended up at his museum.

"So, you want to ask me a couple of questions?"

Yes, of course. This guy was making it too easy. I was searching for paper and pen. Digging through her purse, Jen quickly handed me a notepad and a pencil.

Mr. Irwin spoke to me for more than hour. Not only did I learn about his close friendship with Alex Haley but about Irwin himself. He showed me photos of him and Alex as well as his personal inscribed copies of *Roots* that sat on the bookcase located behind where I was sitting.

"Y'know," Mr. Irwin said in his southern drawl, "that chair you're sitting in, that's where Alex always sat."

I smiled, reclined in the chair and savored the moment.

"I wanna show you something," he told me as he finally lit the cigar that had been dangling from his mouth.

Mr. Irwin rose slowly, touching briefly the desk with his fingertips for balance. He walked over to the conference room where the file cabinets were located.

He pointed to a drawer of one of the cabinets; it was labeled, "Alex Haley."

I asked if I could open it and he nodded in the affirmative.

As I pulled open the drawer, I was in disbelief as my eyes examined hundreds of meticulously organized documents all related to Alex Haley—Haley's will, scores of letters, unpublished manuscripts, travelling schedules, and numerous articles I had yet come across in my research.

Not wanting to overextend my visit, I asked Mr. Irwin if I could come again to peruse his papers.

"Sure," he said nonchalantly.

A month later we returned.

This time I was prepared. Before we arrived at the museum, we drove to Office Max and bought a printer with a copier, several print cartridges, and two reams of paper. I also took along an empty duffle bag for the hundreds of copies I was planning to make.

That day Mr. Irwin and I spoke more about Alex, despite the fact that he was nursing a wound on his arm from a fall that had occurred hours earlier.

Nevertheless, he was still filled with humor and even shared a bottle of his Moonshine. I took a sip and cringed. I felt I had ingested gasoline. With reluctance, I took another sip to show him I wasn't a wussy Yankee.

I wish I could say that Mr. Irwin and I kept in touch, but we didn't. I had sent him a bottle of white wine to thank him for his generosity. We exchanged a couple of letters, but that was all. Life has a way of getting in the way. I had hoped to attend the museum's annual celebration that fall, but was unable to make it.

A year and half after our second visit, Mr. Irwin suffered a stroke. He survived, but currently is living in a nursing home and has limited mobility.

I hope to see Mr. Irwin again and share with him a copy of my book. Maybe he'll put it on his bookshelf, next to *Roots*.

BLACK IN BELFAST

March 11, 2014
https://medium.com/african-american-notes/
857b73335f74

Over the past five years while I was conducting research for *Alex Haley's* Roots: *An Author's Odyssey*, I had the pleasure of interviewing several of Haley's friends, fellow writers, and colleagues.

In 2010, during an interview I conducted with Fulton

Oursler, Jr., a former Reader's Digest editor, he shared several stories about working with Alex Haley.

There was one particular tale that I have always kept in mind.

In the late 1960s, Haley had arrived at the *Digest* campus in Pleasantville, New York, for a luncheon meeting with Oursler and a group of other editors. The author was updating them on his progress with *Roots*.

He had just returned from Ireland. When they inquired about his trip, Haley told the following story.

***

"Follow that road," the Irish innkeeper advised Haley.

The inn was located in Northern Ireland's countryside, where Haley was staying and conducting research about his father's ancestry. Restless, the writer was looking for a place to unwind. The road, he was told, would eventually lead to a tavern.

Haley heeded the innkeeper's advice and went about his way.

After a short amount of time, eventually he found the tavern. When he opened the door, he noticed there were about thirty men and women inside, all of whom, it seemed to Haley, knew one another.

When he walked in and was spotted by a sea of white faces, "there was utter silence."

Gazing at the black man in the entryway, it was as if these people had suddenly suffered from "paralysis." Their eyes were fixated on his every move. Not a word was spoken.

"I have a feeling" Haley thought to himself, "I may have been the only black person they had ever seen in their lives."

Haley walked up to the bar.

"I'd like to have some beer," he told the bartender, who leaned into Haley as he was standing behind the counter.

There was a long, awkward pause before the bartender responded.

"And what church would you be going to?" he asked Haley in his thick brogue, loud enough for all the patrons to hear.

Caught off-guard, Haley didn't know how to respond. The question was the furthest thing from his mind. Here's a man who had endured bitter racism, poverty, bouts with suicide, a broken marriage, and yet, at this moment, for all his real-life experience, he drew a blank.

With nothing clever to come up with, Haley opted for the truth, hoping that would simmer the mood.

My family was Baptist, he divulged.

The mood in the tavern immediately shifted from skepticism to jubilation. Haley was given his drink and all was merry for the remainder of the night. Someone even bought him a beer.

The *Digest* editors, all of whom were white, enjoyed the story but Haley saw that they did not fully get the point he was trying to make.

"They didn't care that I was black," Haley explained to the group. "They just wanted to know what church I went to."

The editors still looked a bit confused.

"The reason I told that story," Haley went on, "[is that] if you ever want to know what it's like to be a nigger, go to Belfast and tell them you're a Catholic!"

IS SELF PUBLISHING A VIABLE ALTERNATIVE FOR BIOGRAPHERS?

April 2014

Originally published in *The Biographer's Craft* newsletter

http://t.e2ma.net/message/pbooe/h59xcc

I knew the odds were stacked against me.

I was neither a professor, nor a journalist, nor an archivist. Put succinctly, I was a bibliophile, who loved history and yearned to become a writer.

My father, a professor emeritus of US history, spent a decade researching and writing a book, yet struggled to secure a publisher. Eventually, he found one, but was disappointed to see how little marketing was provided. It was through his own efforts, for example, arranging numerous book talks and signings, that sales of his book reached respectable numbers, far greater than if he had relied solely on his publisher. Regardless of my father's expenditure of time and energy, his royalty percentage didn't change—he received $3.00 (or 10%) for every book sold. His colleagues, some of whom were contracted by the most prestigious publishers in the industry, also experienced mixed results in terms of marketing, royalties, and dealing with the bureaucracy.

Unless you are a brand name like David McCullough, authors, in most cases, financially and otherwise, are responsible for much of their book's publicity—all for a meager percentage of sales.

Fortunately, in 2014, there is a viable alternative—publish the book yourself.

Once upon a time, it was looked down upon, but no longer. In many respects, Amazon has destigmatized self-publishing, and in the process transformed how we sell books.

With an attractive royalty split (70% goes to the author if your book sells between $2.99 and $9.99; otherwise, it's 35%), flexibility (author determines when the book is available), an infinite shelf life, a seamless publication process, and an incredible customer service (the best I've ever experienced), there is no greater opportunity for lesser-known and unknown authors.

In the last few years, thousands of memoirists, mystery, romance, science fiction, and young adult authors have jumped on the self-publishing bandwagon. Biographers like myself have been slow to embrace the do-it-yourself (DIY) method.

Why?

In the first place, self-publishing (despite its growing popularity) still implies in some circles that your book is not worthy of attracting a publisher. Second, publishers provide an advance to supplement research-related-expenses, such as the cost of airfare, rental car, hotel room, and permissions. (However, the allotment has become smaller and smaller in recent years.) Third, publishers provide publicity. Well, sort of. And finally, publishers also provide access to booksellers. Really? Have you noticed the unfortunate demise of the local and chain brick and mortar bookstores? Borders, anyone?

So, why go "indie" (the preferred title for those who self publish)?

There are several reasons. You determine the length of the book. You have full control of what the cover will look like, choice of editor, setting the price, and the release date. And did I mention the royalty split?

But all is not rosy.

In order for your DIY book to have any chance of success, you must establish a workable budget because you are not only an author, but also a publisher and a marketer (which, as I've explained, you already are when working with a traditional publisher).

From hiring an editor and a book cover designer to securing permission to use copyrighted material and creating your own website, there is plenty of work to be done beyond simply writing.

And that's the easy part.

The hard part: How to get the word out?

Unless you seize the initiative, no one (except for family and close friends) will know where to locate and purchase your book.

Enter social media.

Writers cringe when they hear those words, but to any mid-list or self-published author, Facebook, Goodreads, Twitter, and/or WordPress will quickly become your best friends.

How else are you going to reach readers? Through your newspaper's weekly book review section?

Whether your book is released by a publisher or by you, you're no longer an author, but an entrepreneur.

In the end, the key to your book's success will much depend on your efforts.

BEST PART ABOUT BEING A SELF-PUBLISHED AUTHOR

July 28, 2014
http://adamhenig.com/2014/07/28/best-part-about-being-a-self-published-author/

What's the best part about being a self-published author?

Well, that's easy—selecting your book cover!

One of the biggest gripes among traditional published authors, aside from getting nominal royalty rates, receiving minimal visibility in bookstores, and waiting months (if not years) for your book to be published is that they have no control over one of the most important features of their book—the cover design.

For self-published authors, we can choose any cover design we like or, if we have enough talent, create our own.

One of my editors recommended a professional graphic artist who designed my current book cover.

My plan was to have him use a photograph of Alex Haley, which I had purchased from *Associated Press (AP)* granting me eBook commercial rights for five years. The artist, whom I had hired, did a splendid job, positioning the photograph, title, and my name on the cover.

He charged his standard fee for a single design. If I wanted another design, there would be an additional fee.

Six months later, when I began thinking about publishing a paperback edition of my eBook, I investigated the cost of publishing the same photograph on a hard cover. To my chagrin, *AP* charged about the same fee I had paid to have the image on my eBook cover.

Furthermore, I would have to pay my designer another fee just to create a back cover (since there wasn't one prior).

And I would have to renew the rights to the photograph every five years.

At that point, I had all but given up on publishing a book I could actually hold in my hands and turn the page.

Then, it occurred to me while I was listening to my favorite podcast program on writing—Self-Publishing Podcast—that there was a plausible alternative.

The podcast is hosted by three indie authors—Sean

Platt, Johnny B. Truant, and David W. Wright. It was their lone sponsor, 99 Designs, who caught my attention.

99 Designs is a San Francisco-based web company that provides a marketplace for graphic designers to showcase their work based on a business' needs.

The designers compete in a contest (paid for by a business or an individual), and, whichever design is selected by the person(s) paying for the service, the winning artist receives two-thirds of the fee. 99 Designs takes the other third.

The best part about working with 99 Designs is that there is no obligation if you don't like any of the designs. You'll receive a full refund.

Although the concept seemed perfect for my situation, I was convinced when Wright said on Episode #109: "We're not going to advertise anything on this site that we would not use....If you want a professional design, go to 99 Designs."

I filled out an application (where I explained what I was looking for in a book cover), paid my $299 fee, and watched the submissions roll in.

At first, there were only a few and they weren't eye-catching. I began to wonder if I had made a mistake. But by the following morning, scores had been submitted and there were enough quality designs in the lot that I knew a refund would not be necessary. By the end of the seven-day-period, I received a total of 145 submissions in the opening round! At least twenty of them I deemed "cover worthy" and those made it to the final round.

Of those, I narrowed it down to eight designs, and then I asked my readers to choose the one they liked best.

Although the decision, in the end, was mine, I conducted the poll for a reason. As David Wright reminded me, I "gotta please the masses" because they are the ones that will ultimately purchase my book.

Designer Rachmad Agus received the most votes, not surprisingly given his success on other projects. Rachmad and I worked together to make the final touch-ups on the cover.

Once completed, the final piece of the puzzle was put into place. Yet my journey as a self published author is far from over.

After all, my book is as much about Alex Haley as it is about discovering the art of self-publishing in the digital age. Today's self-publishing profession is still in the incubation stage, but one thing is certain: numerous authors from around the world have demonstrated that it's not a fad or a phenomenon. It's a serious business, which allows writers to bypass traditional publishing houses and let the reading public determine the merit of their work.

ACKNOWLEDGEMENTS

This book would not have come to fruition without the guidance and inspiration of my father, Gerald S. Henig, emeritus professor of history. He scrutinized every sentence of the manuscript, occasionally questioning my interpretation of the evidence, and oftentimes holding me to task for lack of clarity. From scanning files to conducting genealogical research of Alex Haley's family, my mother, Lori Henig, was incredibly helpful.

There were a number of research institutions and universities that offered assistance in either retrieving the documents I requested or providing me access to the papers themselves. No staff was more helpful than the University of Tennessee, Knoxville, John C. Hodges Library, Special Collections Division—Jennifer Benedetto Beals, Nick Wyman, Justin Blake Eastwood, Elizabeth Campbell Young, and Bill Eigelsbach as well as student researcher Zach Johnson. The Anne Romaine Papers in the special collections shed enormous insight on Haley's life.

Also, I would like to acknowledge the following research institutions and persons for their support: Alcorn University (Joanna Williams), Atlanta University Center (Kayin Shabazz), Clark Atlanta University (Kashawndros

Jackson), Columbia University (Catherine Carson Ricciardi), Cornell University (Evan Fay Earle, Annie Keville), Duke University (Lynn Eaton), California State University, East Bay (Carolyn Chun, Jared Mariconi), Georgetown University (Scott S. Taylor), Hamilton College (Katherine Collett), Jackson State University (Angela Stewart), Lane College (Lan Wang), Langston University (Jovanni Williams), Library of Congress (Alice Birney, Bonnie Coles), University of Michigan, Ann Arbor (Kate Hutchens), University of North Carolina at Chapel Hill (staff at the Louis Round Wilson Special Collections Library), San Jose Public Library (staff), Santa Clara County Library (staff), University of California, Santa Cruz (Luisa Haddad), Saratoga Springs Public Library (Teri Blasko), Schomburg Center for Research in Black Culture (Edwina Ashie-Nikoi and staff), Skidmore College (Wendy Anthony), Syracuse University (Mary Beth Hinton, Lauren M. Britton, Sean Quimby, Nicolette A. Dobrowolski, Jessica O'Toole), Tennessee Historical Commission (Claudette Stager), Thought Equity Motion (Linzey Simonson) and Vanderbilt University (Molly Dohrmann).

Interviews are never easy to arrange. Despite setbacks, there were people in Alex Haley's life that generously volunteered their time while sharing their most intimate memories. Among them, Haley's best friend, Museum of Appalachia founder and writer/historian/archivist John Rice Irwin.

To other Tennesseans who knew Haley—Edye Ellis, Girdie King and her husband, Kathy Stooksbury-Long, and Nick Wyman—I owe a debt of gratitude for their insight and anecdotes. I am also grateful to Ken Libby, Business Manager of the Children's Defense Fund, which owns the Haley Farm, for providing access to the facility; William Vincent Murray, Director of Alamance County Museum, who responded to numerous questions; and Donna Banks of *Reader's Digest*, who led me to Haley's former *Digest* editors, Ed Thompson and Fulton Oursler, Jr., who were generous with their time and insights. Finally, Michael Courlander, son of Harold Courlander, not only granted me access to his father's personal papers but made himself available for an interview.

Furthermore, I would like to express my appreciation to the always congenial baristas at the Starbucks' Stores in San Jose (#12673 & #15255), and my gratitude to Norma Garcia for sharing her marketing expertise.

I was most fortunate to be the beneficiary of the professional editorial skills of Barbara Alexandra (Alex) Szerlip. Alex did not hold back any of her criticism, often bluntly telling me what was wrong and then following up with a solution, or, at the very least, a suggestion. Her keen editorial eye truly saved me from countless stylistic blunders. Also, I would like to express my deep gratitude to Amy Quale for her invaluable editorial insight and assistance. My thanks as well to the very talented Rachmad Agus for designing the cover.

I am most grateful to my sisters, Jennifer and Rebecca, and to my nieces, brothers-in-law, sisters-in-law, fathers-in-law and mothers in-law, and friends for their good cheer and encouragement.

Finally, and most importantly, my wife (and fellow researcher), Jennifer, and my sons, Jacob and Alexander, are the angels in my life.

ABOUT THE AUTHOR

Born and raised in the San Francisco Bay Area, Adam Henig attended California State University, Chico, majoring in political science with an emphasis in cultural and international studies. After graduation, he pursued his interest in African American history and literature.

Alex Haley's Roots: *An Author's Odyssey* is his first publication. A book reviewer and blogger, Adam's writings have appeared in the *San Francisco Book Review, Portland Book Review, Tulsa Book Review, The Indie Writer Network Daily, Medium, The Biographer's Craft,* and *Blogcritics.* He's also been featured on the podcast, *New Books Network: African American Studies.* Adam is an active member of the Biographers International Group (BIO).

If you would like to read more about Adam's literary activities, visit www.adamhenig.com and subscribe to his blog.

The author can be reached at info@adamhenig.com or follow him on Twitter @adamhenig.